LONGMAN LITERATURE SHAKESPEARE

The Merchant of Venice

William Shakespeare

Editor: Laura Hutchings

 LONGMAN

Longman Literature Shakespeare

Series editor: Roy Blatchford
Consultant: Jackie Head

Macbeth   0 582 08827 5 (paper)
             0 582 24592 3 (cased)
Romeo and Juliet   0 582 08836 4 (paper)
                 0 582 24591 5 (cased)
The Merchant of Venice   0 582 08835 6 (paper)
                     0 582 24593 1 (cased)
A Midsummer Night's Dream   0 582 08833 X (paper)
                       0 582 24590 7 (cased)
Julius Caesar   0 582 08828 3 (paper)
              0 582 24589 3 (cased)
Twelfth Night   0 582 08834 8 (paper)
Othello   0 582 09719 3 (paper)
King Lear   0 582 09718 5 (paper)
Hamlet   0 582 09720 7 (paper)

Longman Literature

Series editor: Roy Blatchford

Plays

Alan Ayckbourn   *Absurd Person Singular*   0 582 06020 6
Arthur Miller   *An Enemy of the People*   0 582 09717 7
J B Priestley   *An Inspector Calls*   0 582 06012 5
Terence Rattigan   *The Winslow Boy*   0 582 06019 2
Willy Russell   *Educating Rita*   0 582 06013 3
               Shirley Valentine   0 582 08173 4
Peter Shaffer   *The Royal Hunt of the Sun*   0 582 06014 1
               Equus   0 582 09712 6
Bernard Shaw   *Arms and the Man*   0 582 07785 0
               Pygmalion   0 582 06015 X
               Saint Joan   0 582 07786 9
Oscar Wilde   *The Importance of Being Earnest*   0 582 07784 2

Other titles in the Longman Literature series are listed on page 284.

Contents

Introduction

Shakespeare's life and times

Shakespeare was born into a time of change. Important discoveries about the world were changing people's whole way of life, their thoughts and their beliefs. The fact that we know very little of Shakespeare's particular life story does not mean that we cannot step into his world.

What do we know about Shakespeare?

Imagine for a minute you are Shakespeare, born in 1564, the son of a businessman who is making his way in Stratford-upon-Avon. When you are thirteen, Francis Drake sets off on a dangerous sea voyage around the world, to prove that it is round, not flat, and to bring back riches. The trades people who pass in and out of your town bring with them stories of other countries, each with their own unique culture and language. You learn in school of ancient heroic myths taught through Latin and Greek, and often, to bring these stories alive, travelling theatres pass through the town acting, singing, performing, and bringing with them tales of London. But, at the age of fourteen your own world shifts a little under your feet; your father has got into serious debt, you find yourself having to grow up rather fast.

This is an unremarkable life so far – the death of your sisters is not an uncommon occurrence at this time, and even when you marry at eighteen, your bride already pregnant at the ceremony, you are not the first to live through life in this way. After your daughter, your wife gives birth to twins, a girl and a boy, one of whom dies when he is eleven. But before this, for some reason only you know, perhaps to do with some poaching you are involved in or because your marriage to a woman eight years older than you is having difficulties, you travel to London. There you eventually join the theatre, first as an actor and then as a writer. You write for the theatres in the inn yards, then for Queen Elizabeth in court, and when she dies, for King James I. As well as this you write for the large theatres which are being built in London: the Rose, the Globe, Blackfriars and the Swan. You die a rich man.

What did Shakespeare find in London?

When Shakespeare first travelled to London he found a city full of all that was best and worst in this new era of discovery. There was trade in expensive and fashionable items, a bubbling street life with street-theatre, pedlars of every sort, sellers of songs and poems. Industry was flourishing in textiles, mining, the manufacture of glass, iron, and sugar. The place to be known was the court of Queen Elizabeth. She was unmarried and drew many admirers even in her old age, maintaining a dazzling social world with her at its centre. There were writers and poets, grasping what they could of the new world, building on the literature of other countries, charting the lingering death of medieval life and the chaotic birth of something new.

By contrast, Shakespeare also found poverty, death and disease. The plague, spread by rats, found an easy home in these narrow streets, often spilling over with dirt and sewage: it killed 15,000 people in London in 1592 alone. It was an overcrowded city: the increased demand for wool for trade brought about the enclosure of land in the countryside, and this, coupled with bad harvests, brought the peasants, thrown off their land and made poor, into London to seek wealth.

What was England like in Shakespeare's day?

England was a proud nation. Elizabeth would not tolerate rivals and destroyed her enemies. In 1587 she had Mary Queen of Scots executed for treason, and in 1588 her navy defeated a huge armada of ships from Spain. Both acts were prompted by religion. In maintaining the Protestant Church of England her father, King Henry VIII, had established, Elizabeth stood out against a strong Catholic Europe. Within the Protestant religion too, there were divisions, producing extreme groups such as the Puritans who believed that much of the Elizabethan social scene was sinful, the theatres being one of their clearest targets for disapproval. Her power was threatened for other reasons too. In 1594 her doctor was executed for attempting to poison her, and in 1601 one of her favourites, the Earl of Essex, led an unsuccessful revolt against her.

When Elizabeth died in 1603 and James I succeeded her, he brought a change. He was a Scottish king, and traditionally Scotland and England had had an uneasy relationship. He was interested in witchcraft and he supported the arts, but not in the same way as Elizabeth had. He too met with treason, in the shape of Guy Fawkes and his followers, who in 1605 attempted to blow up The Houses of Parliament. If Shakespeare needed examples of life at its extremes, he had them all around him, and his closeness to the court meant he understood them more than most.

What other changes did Shakespeare see?

Towards the end of Shakespeare's life, in Italy, a man Shakespeare's age invented the telescope and looked at the stars. His radical discoveries caused him to be thrown out of the Catholic Church. For fifteen centuries people had believed in a picture of the universe as held in crystal spheres with order and beauty, and everything centring around the earth. In this belief the sun, moon and stars were the heavens; they ruled human fate, they were distant and magical. Galileo proved this was not so. So, the world was no longer flat and the earth was not the centre of the universe. It must have felt as if nothing was to be trusted anymore.

What do Shakespeare's plays show us about Elizabethan life?

Even without history books much of Shakespeare's life can be seen in his plays. They are written by one who knows of the tragedy of sudden death, and illness, and of the splendour of the life of the court in contrast to urban and rural poverty. He knows the ancient myths of the Greeks and Romans, the history of change in his own country, and, perhaps from reading the translations carried by merchants to London, he knows the literature of Spain and Italy.

His plays also contain all the hustle and bustle of normal life at the time. We see the court fool, the aristocracy, royalty, merchants and the servant classes. We hear of bear-baiting, fortune-telling, entertaining, drinking, dancing and singing. As new changes happen they are brought into the plays, in the form of maps, clocks, or the latest fashions. Shakespeare wrote to perform, and his plays were performed to bring financial reward. He studied his audience closely and produced what they wanted. Sometimes, as with the focus on witchcraft in *Macbeth* written for King James I, this was the celebration of something which fascinated them; sometimes, as with the character of Malvolio in *Twelfth Night*, it was the mockery of something they despised.

What do Shakespeare's plays tell us about life now?

You can read Shakespeare's plays to find out about Elizabethan life, but in them you will also see reflected back at you the unchanging aspects of humanity. It is as if in all that changed around him, Shakespeare looked for the things that would *not* change – like love, power, honour, friendship and loyalty – and put them to the test. In each he found strength and weakness.

We see *love*:
- at first sight,
- which is one-sided,
- between young lovers,
- in old age,
- between members of one family,
- lost and found again.

We see *power*:
- used and abused,
- in those who seek it,
- in those who protect it with loyalty,
- in the just and merciful rule of wise leaders,
- in the hands of wicked tyrants.

We see *honour*:
- in noble men and women,
- lost through foolishness,
- stolen away through trickery and disloyalty.

We see *friendship*:

- between men and men, women and women, men and women,
- between masters and servants,
- put to the test of jealousy, grief and misunderstanding.

These are just some examples of how Shakespeare explored in his plays what it was to be human. He lived for fifty-two years and wrote thirty-seven plays, as well as a great number of poems. Just in terms of output this is a remarkable achievement. What is even more remarkable is the way in which he provides a window for his audiences into all that is truly human, and it is this quality that often touches us today.

What are Comedies, Tragedies and Histories?

When Shakespeare died, his players brought together the works he had written, and had them published. Before this some of the plays had only really existed as actors' scripts written for their parts alone. Many plays in Shakespeare's day and before were not written down at all, but spoken, and kept in people's memories from generation to generation. So, making accurate copies of Shakespeare's plays was not easy and there is still some dispute over how close to the original scripts our current editions are. Ever since they were first published people have tried to make sense of them. Sometimes they are described under three headings: Comedy, Tragedy and History. The dates on the chart that follows refer to the dates of the first recorded performances or, if this is not known, the date of first publication. They may have been performed earlier but history has left us no record; dating the plays exactly is therefore difficult.

COMEDY	HISTORY	TRAGEDY
	King John (1590)	
	Henry VI, Part I (1592)	
Comedy of Errors (1594) The Taming of the Shrew (1594) Two Gentlemen of Verona (1594)		Titus Andronicus (1594)
The Merry Wives of Windsor (1597)	Richard II (1597) Richard III (1597)	Romeo and Juliet (1597)
The Merchant of Venice (1598) Love's Labour's Lost (1598)	Henry IV, Part II (1598)	
As You Like It (1600) A Midsummer Night's Dream (1600) Much Ado About Nothing (1600) Twelfth Night (1600) Troilus and Cressida (1601)	Henry V (1600) Henry VI, Part II (1600) Henry VI, Part III (1600)	
		Hamlet (1602)
Measure for Measure (1604) All's Well That Ends Well (1604)	Henry IV, Part I (1604)	Othello (1604)

COMEDY	HISTORY	TRAGEDY
		Julius Caesar (1605)
		Macbeth (1606)
		King Lear (1606)
		Antony and Cleopatra (1608)
		Timon of Athens (1608)
		Coriolanus (1608)
Pericles (1609)		
Cymbeline (1611)		
The Winter's Tale (1611)		
The Tempest (1612)	Henry VIII (1612)	

Comedy = a play which maintains a thread of joy throughout and ends happily for most of its characters.

Tragedy = a play in which characters must struggle with circumstances and in which most meet death and despair.

History = a play focusing on a real event or series of events which actually happened in the past.

These three headings can be misleading. Many of the comedies have great sadness in them, and there is humour in most of the tragedies, some of which at least point to happier events in the future. Some of the tragedies, like *Macbeth* and *Julius Caesar*, make history their starting point.

We do not know exactly when each play was written but from what we know of when they were performed we can see that Shakespeare began by writing poetry, then histories and comedies. He wrote most of his tragedies in the last ten years of his life, and in his final writings wrote stories full of near-tragic problems which, by the end of the plays he resolved. Sometimes these final plays (*Pericles*, *Cymbeline*, *The Winter's Tale* and *The Tempest*) are called Comedies, sometimes they are called Romances or simply The Problem Plays.

Where were Shakespeare's plays performed?

Plays in Shakespeare's day were performed in several places, not just in specially designed theatres.

Inn Yard Theatre: Players performed in the open courtyard of Elizabethan inns. These were places where people could drink, eat and stay the night. They were popular places to make a break in a journey and to change or rest horses. Some inns built a permanent platform in the yard, and the audience could stand in the yard itself, or under shelter in the galleries which overlooked the yard. The audiences were lively and used to the active entertainment of bear-baiting, cock-fighting, wrestling and juggling. Plays performed here needed to be action-packed and appealing to a wide audience. In 1574 new regulations were made to control performances in response to the number of fights which regularly broke out in the audience.

Private House Theatre: The rich lords of Elizabethan times would pay travelling theatre companies to play in the large rooms of their own private houses for the benefit of their friends. There was no stage and the audience were all seated. Torches and candles were used to create artificial lighting. Costumes played an important part in creating atmosphere but there were no sets.

Public Hall Theatre: Some town councils would allow performances of plays in their grand halls and council buildings. As well as this, ceremonial halls such as the Queen's courts in Whitehall were frequently used in this way, as were halls at Hampton Court, Richmond and Greenwich Palace. For these performances, designed for a larger audience than those given in private houses, scaffolding would be arranged for tiered seating which would surround a central acting area. Audiences were limited to those with a high social standing.

Public Theatres: Unlike Public Hall theatres, these theatres were built for the purpose of presenting plays. At the end of the sixteenth century there were about 200,000 people living in London, and eleven public theatres showing performances. Of these, about half a dozen were so large that they seated about 2,000 people. The audiences, who were drawn from all sections of society, paid to see performances which began at 2 p.m. The audience sat in covered galleries around a circular acting area which was open air. Whilst the theatres stood within the City of London they were subject to its laws. They could not perform during times of worship, and they were closed during outbreaks of the plague. Theatres were often the scenes of fighting and because of the trouble this caused, in 1596 performances of plays were forbidden within the city boundaries. So people started building theatres outside the city on the south side of the River Thames.

What were the performances like?

To some extent this depended on the play being performed and the audience watching. A play performed before the court of the queen or king would need to be one that did not offend the ruler. Plays performed in the inn yard or the public theatres needed to have a wide appeal and several distractions such as dancing and music to keep the audience's attention.

Wherever they performed, the players had to create the illusion that the whole world could be seen inside their play. They had no sets, except in some cases tapestries which were hung up to show changes in scenery, but they did have bright costumes in which to perform. Scenes of battle or shipwreck were suggested by words rather than special effects, though we do know that they used burning torches, as it was due to a fire caused by one of these that the first Globe Theatre burnt down during a performance in 1613.

Actors joined together in companies, who would perform several different plays, and be sponsored by the nobility. Shakespeare became a key member of the Lord Chamberlain's company which Queen Elizabeth sponsored, and which went on to be called The King's Men when James I became king.

There were no women on the Elizabethan stage. Most female characters would be played by boys whose voices had not yet broken, or if it was an old character, by men in the company. Actors carried a reputation for being immoral and ungodly people, and were therefore thought unsuitable company for women. The men of Shakespeare's company became famous for playing particular types of characters such as the fool, the lover or the villain. Shakespeare probably created many of his parts with particular actors in mind.

Where can I find out more about Shakespeare?

Shakespeare is perhaps the world's most famous playwright and there is no shortage of books written about him. In your library or bookshop you will find books which look at:

- Shakespeare's life;
- the history of England under the reign of Queen Elizabeth I and James I;
- European history, art and literature of the sixteenth and seventeenth century;
- discoveries made throughout the world during Elizabethan times;
- characters, themes and ideas in Shakespeare's writing.

In Stratford-upon-Avon, where Shakespeare was born you can visit his birthplace, and much of the town consists of buildings which would have stood in Shakespeare's day. In addition to this there are many museums and exhibitions which tell more about Shakespeare's life and work.

Some theatrical companies today, such as the Royal Shakespeare Company, devote themselves to performing Shakespeare's plays in London, Stratford, and on tour around the country. They are always seeking new ways to bring the plays to life. However, perhaps the best way to find out more about Shakespeare is to study his plays by reading and acting them yourself and by seeing them in performance. Shakespeare wrote about what he knew, and the key to discovering how his mind and emotions worked is to look at what he wrote.

Shakespeare's language

Reading Shakespeare

The first thing to remember when studying any of Shakespeare's plays is that they were not designed to be read silently to yourself, like a novel. To be appreciated properly they should really be seen - but even reading the lines aloud can help you understand parts of the play that you might otherwise have trouble with.

It is not always easy reading lines that were written almost 400 years ago. A lot of the words that Shakespeare uses have either changed their meaning now, or are no longer used at all. Sometimes he uses difficult vocabulary that you will not have come across before.

Look at the two speeches that open the play. The language in both these speeches can cause problems for different reasons. How many of the words in this speech of Antonio's are 'old' words that we no longer use?

ANTONIO
> In sooth, I know not why I am so sad;
> It wearies me; you say it wearies you;
> But how I caught it, found it, or came by it,
> What stuff't is made of, whereof it is born,
> I am to learn;
> And such a want-wit sadness makes of me
> That I have much ado to know myself.

(Act 1, scene 1, lines 1–7)

Now look at Salerio's reply. What problems might you have in reading and understanding this speech?

SALERIO
> Your mind is tossing on the ocean,
> There where your argosies with portly sail,
> Like signiors and rich burghers on the flood,
> Or as it were the pageants of the sea,
> Do overpeer the petty traffickers
> That curtsey to them, do them reverence,
> As they fly by them with their woven wings.

(Act 1, scene 1, lines 8–14)

As you become more familiar with Shakespeare you will find yourself recognising a lot of the 'old' words without having to look them up. However, the glossary is there to help you with words and phrases you do not understand,

and here are some more ways to work out the meanings:

- Are the words similar to modern words, can you guess their meaning from this?

- Is there a general theme in the conversation or speech, that might give you some clues?

- Where and when is this scene taking place? What is the main action? Can you picture the scene and pick up clues from the setting?

- What are the characters like? When a character reappears, think about how they were before: were they funny, depressed, scared, serious? Can you guess at the sort of things this person might say and the sort of tone they are likely to adopt?

Don't worry if you don't understand every word. On your first reading, what is important is getting the gist of what is being said.

Having looked at the vocabulary that Shakespeare uses, the next step is to think about reading his lines aloud. Fortunately, there are some rules that make life easier:

- Look for the punctuation. It is here that you should stop and take a breath.

- Try not to take too much notice of the fact that a lot of the play is set out like poetry. Follow the sentences, not the lines, to get the meaning.

- Try to work out the meaning of what you are saying. If you concentrate on trying to get that meaning across to those listening, you will find that things like emphasis on words and the correct place to pause will take care of themselves.

- Finally, it is difficult to get Shakespeare right if you are reading it for the first time. We all make mistakes when we sight-read even ordinary pieces of prose. If you have the chance, read through the section of the play that you are about to study beforehand. It helps too if you do this reading aloud.

Blank verse

By the time Shakespeare came to write his plays it had become the fashion for drama to be written in *blank verse*. Blank verse is the name given to a type of poetry that does not have to rhyme, and that has ten beats to a line. Read the following speech out loud and get a partner to count the beats.

BASSANIO

    In Belmont is a lady richly left,
    And she is fair, and, fairer than that word,
    Of wondrous virtues. Sometimes from her eyes
    I did receive fair speechless messages.

(Act 1, scene 1, lines 161-4)

How many beats are there to each line? Which words are stressed (which words do you automatically put emphasis on when you read them), and which words are not stressed? You should find that you can pair up the stressed and the unstressed words. How many pairs do you have?

Before we go on to look at how Shakespeare varies his blank verse from time to time, it is worth going back to Antonio's opening speech to look at one other detail. The first word in a line of poetry usually begins with a capital letter, and blank verse is no exception. So, despite the fact that there is only one full stop in this speech, there are actually seven lines beginning with capital letters. Remember the rules for reading Shakespeare. Look for the commas and full stops and try to read the lines as sentences rather than separate lines of verse.

Although blank verse is a very good way of writing a play, you can have too much of a good thing! To keep his audience (and his actors!) paying attention Shakespeare varies the way in which he writes from time to time. Sometimes he breaks the line up so that two characters share one complete line of verse. In the following example Bassanio finishes Shylock's line:

SHYLOCK

                    ... cursed be my tribe
    If I forgive him!

BASSANIO

                Shylock, do you hear?

(Act 1, scene 3, lines 47–9)

Sometimes, in order to get the correct rhythm, words are shortened. In the following speech of Lorenzo's three words have had letters missed out so that the middle line keeps its regular beat of ten syllables:

LORENZO
> No, pray thee, let it serve for table-talk;
> Then, howsome'er thou speak'st, 'mong other things
> I shall digest it.

(Act 3, scene 5, lines 83–5)

With the letters left in, the line would read: 'Then, howsomever thou speakest. among other things', which would spoil the rhythm completely.

Similarly, you have to make sure that 'ed' at the end of a word is pronounced as a separate syllable when it is necessary to keep the rhythm, as in this example from one of Portia's speeches. The word 'establishèd' is given an accent to remind you to pronounce the 'ed' separately:

PORTIA
> It must not be; there is no power in Venice
> Can alter a decree establishèd...

(Act 4, scene 1, lines 214–5)

The most obvious way in which Shakespeare keeps our interest, however, is simply by letting his characters speak in prose occasionally. There are no hard and fast rules for exactly where you will find prose in his plays. Generally servants, such as Launcelot and Nerissa, use prose while people of a higher class use verse, but this is not always the case. Look, for example, at the beginning of Act 1, scene 3. Here, Shylock begins by speaking in prose but when Antonio appears on the scene Shylock moves into blank verse. Look out for similar changes in the rest of the play. Remember that the most powerful and the most moving speeches of the play are those written in verse.

Do the changes from prose to verse help us to see what Shakespeare thought were the important issues of the play?

Poetry

Because Shakespeare was not only a playwright, but also a very great poet, and because much of *The Merchant of Venice* is written in verse, it is natural that some of the literary devices that you would expect to find in poetry can also be found in the play. Probably the most powerful of these devices is Shakespeare's use of images, similes and metaphors. These all help to paint 'word-pictures' that create, or add to, the meaning of what is being said.

If we go back to Salerio's speech at the beginning of the play we can see that by comparing Antonio's ships to noblemen and rich merchants, and by saying that the smaller ships 'curtsy to them', he is telling us that Antonio himself is a wealthy and important man who can afford grand ships and the precious cargoes that they carry. Not only does he do this, but he also paints a charming picture of the busy sea lanes of Elizabethan times – all this in just seven lines of verse! As you read through the play watch out for such images; in particular you will find several references to money and money-lending. These references can turn up in some unusual places. Here, for example, Portia tells her future husband, Bassanio, just how much she loves him:

PORTIA

> You see me, Lord Bassanio, where I stand,
> Such as I am; though for myself alone
> I would not be ambitious in my wish
> To wish myself much better, yet for you,
> I would be trebled twenty times myself,
> A thousand times more fair, ten thousand times
>   more rich,
> That only to stand high in your account,
> I might in virtues, beauties, livings, friends
> Exceed account. But the full sum of me
> Is sum of – something: which, to term in gross,
> Is an unlessoned girl, unschooled, unpractised...

(Act 3, scene 2, lines 149–59)

Throughout the play, even when watching the scenes set in Belmont, we are constantly being reminded of the fact that the main plot revolves around a bargain made for money. By the end of the play, Antonio has committed himself once again to seeing that another (very different) kind of agreement is carried out. As you read *The Merchant of Venice* see how many of these echoes of the main plot you can find.

The Elizabethans were very fond of playing with language and they delighted in puns and verbal jokes. Of course, some of the humour has been lost with the passage of time (will anyone laugh at our jokes in 400 years' time?) but much of it remains as witty as when it was first written.

Launcelot Gobbo is the clown of the play and he is an expert when it comes to using words either to amuse himself or to confuse others. Here, he deliberately gives his old father confusing directions:

LAUNCELOT

Turn up on your right hand at the next turning, but at the next turning of all on your left; marry, at the very next turning turn of no hand, but turn down indirectly to the Jew's house.

(Act 2, scene 2, lines 39–42)

As you might expect, he can prove a tiresome servant and later in the play he sorely tries Lorenzo's patience:

LORENZO

How every fool can play upon the word! I think the best grace of wit will shortly turn into silence, and discourse grow commendable in none only but parrots. – Go in, sirrah; bid them prepare for dinner!

LAUNCELOT

That is done, sir; they have all stomachs!

LORENZO

Goodly Lord, what a wit-snapper are you!

(Act 3, scene 5, lines 41–6)

It is not just Launcelot who indulges himself in word games, however. Take a look at this extract from one of Shylock's speeches where he talks about the dangers that might befall a ship at sea:

SHYLOCK

But ships are but boards, sailors but men; there be land-rats and water-rats, water-thieves, and land-thieves, (I mean pirates), and then there is the peril of waters, winds, and rocks...

(Act 1, scene 3, lines 19–23)

There is a lot to think about as you read Shakespeare's plays, and it is for precisely this reason that people return to them time and time again. You will not find everything that *The Merchant of Venice* contains when you read it for the first time, but now you should have some idea of what to look out for. Any notes that you make as you read through the play will help you with the 'Study programme' which follows the play on page 253.

The most important point to keep in mind, however, is that Shakespeare wrote his plays in order to entertain people. It is true that he teaches us a lot whilst he entertains us, but in the end the plays are there to be enjoyed. Your studies should help you to appreciate the richness of the text.

The glossary: a word of warning

The glossary has been compiled to help you understand the language of the play. On occasions complex and beautiful poetry has been translated or paraphrased into mundane, straightforward prose. When this happens, some of the original meaning is bound to be lost. You are advised, therefore, to use the glossary as a help with your first reading, but once you feel you have the main gist of the meaning, you should try to rely on it less.

The Merchant of
Venice

CHARACTERS
in the play

THE DUKE OF VENICE
THE PRINCE OF MOROCCO ⎱ *suitors to Portia*
THE PRINCE OF ARRAGON ⎰
ANTONIO, *a merchant of Venice*
BASSANIO, *his friend, and a suitor to Portia*
GRATIANO ⎫
SALERIO ⎬ *friends of Antonio and Bassanio*
SOLANIO ⎭
LORENZO, *in love with Jessica*
SHYLOCK, *a Jew*
TUBAL, *a Jew, his friend*
LAUNCELOT GOBBO, *the clown of the play, Shylock's servant*
OLD GOBBO, *Launcelot's father*
LEONARDO, *Bassanio's servant*
BALTHAZAR ⎱ *Portia's servants*
STEPHANO ⎰

PORTIA, *an heiress, mistress of Belmont*
NERISSA, *her maid*
JESSICA, *Shylock's daughter*

RICH MERCHANTS OF VENICE, OFFICERS OF THE COURT
OF JUSTICE, A GAOLER, SERVANTS, AND OTHER
ATTENDANTS

The scenes are laid in Venice, and Portia's house at Belmont.

Act 1: summary

We are introduced to Antonio, 'the merchant of Venice'. Although he has his own troubles, Antonio is more than willing to listen when his friend Bassanio comes to him asking for help. Bassanio wishes to travel to Belmont to try to win the hand of Portia, a wealthy heiress living there. In order to make the right impression when he arrives in Belmont Bassanio needs money, but he is already heavily in debt to Antonio. He asks for a second loan and is told that, whilst Antonio is only too willing to help him, unfortunately all his money is tied up in his fleet of sailing ships. Antonio therefore suggests that they borrow money.

Bassanio approaches Shylock, a Jewish moneylender. Shylock hates Antonio, both because he is a Christian and because in the past Antonio has spoilt some of Shylock's business ventures. Nevertheless, he agrees to lend Antonio the sum of 3000 ducats (gold coins) for three months. In exchange for this loan he demands that Antonio signs a contract stating that if he finds himself unable to repay the money he will allow Shylock to cut off a pound of his flesh. Antonio is surprised by the nature of the bargain but agrees to it.

Meanwhile, in Belmont, Portia finds herself honour-bound by the conditions of her dead father's will to marry the first man who correctly solves a riddle concerning three caskets. Portia, talking with her maid Nerissa, discusses with some disgust the men who have turned up so far. Fortunately none of them has solved the puzzle and so, for the moment, she is safe.

(Opposite) Alec Guinness as Shylock in the Chichester Festival Theatre production of The Merchant of Venice, 1984.

1 *In sooth*   in truth.

4 *whereof*   what (it is born) from.

6 *want-wit*   idiot.

7 *I have...myself*   I'm having trouble recognising myself.

9 *argosies*   large merchant ships.

   portly   majestic.

10 *signiors and rich burghers*   gentlemen and rich merchants.

11 *pageants*   colourful displays presented on mobile platforms.

12 *overpeer*   loom over.

   petty traffickers   little trading vessels.

13 *do them reverence*   show them respect.

14 *woven wings*   sails.

15 *such venture forth*   such a fleet at sea.

16 *affections*   awareness.

18 *where sits the wind*   which way the wind blows.

21 *out of doubt*   without a doubt.

Act One

Scene one

Venice. A street.

Enter ANTONIO, SALERIO, *and* SOLANIO.

ANTONIO

    In sooth, I know not why I am so sad;
    It wearies me; you say it wearies you;
    But how I caught it, found it, or came by it,
    What stuff't is made of, whereof it is born,
    I am to learn;   5
    And such a want-wit sadness makes of me
    That I have much ado to know myself.

SALERIO

    Your mind is tossing on the ocean,
    There where your argosies with portly sail,
    Like signiors and rich burghers on the flood,   10
    Or as it were the pageants of the sea,
    Do overpeer the petty traffickers
    That curtsy to them, do them reverence,
    As they fly by them with their woven wings.

SOLANIO

    Believe me, sir, had I such venture forth,   15
    The better part of my affections would
    Be with my hopes abroad. I should be still
    Plucking the grass to know where sits the wind,
    Peering in maps for ports, and piers, and roads;
    And every object that might make me fear   20
    Misfortune to my venture out of doubt
    Would make me sad.

23 *ague*   fever.

26 *flats*   sandbanks.

27 *Andrew*   the name of a ship.

28–9 *Vailing...burial*   rolling on to its side so that the hull is in the air and the masts 'kiss' the sandbank that has caused the wreck.

30 *edifice*   grand building.

31 *bethink me straight*   think straight away.

34 *Enrobe*   dress.

35–6 *in a word...nothing*   becoming instantly worthless.

38 *bechanced*   occurring.

42 *one bottom*   one ship.

43 *estate*   the whole of Antonio's wealth.

46 *Fie, fie!*   rubbish!

SALERIO

                           My wind cooling my broth
Would blow me to an ague when I thought
What harm a wind too great might do at sea.
I should not see the sandy hour-glass run   25
But I should think of shallows and of flats,
And see my wealthy Andrew docked in sand,
Vailing her high top lower than her ribs
To kiss her burial; should I go to church
And see the holy edifice of stone   30
And not bethink me straight of dangerous rocks,
Which touching but my gentle vessel's side
Would scatter all her spices on the stream,
Enrobe the roaring waters with my silks,
And, in a word, but even now worth this,   35
And now worth nothing? Shall I have the thought
To think on this, and shall I lack the thought
That such a thing bechanced would make me sad?
But tell not me, I know Antonio
Is sad to think upon his merchandise.   40

ANTONIO

Believe me no, I thank my fortune for it –
My ventures are not in one bottom trusted,
Nor to one place; nor is my whole estate
Upon the fortune of this present year;
Therefore my merchandise makes me not sad.   45

SOLANIO

Why then, you are in love.

ANTONIO

Fie, fie!

SOLANIO

Not in love neither; then let us say you are sad

9

50   *Janus*   two-faced (literally) Roman god of doorways; one face smiled and the other frowned.

51   *framed*   created.

53   *laugh like parrots at a bagpiper*   something very silly laughing at something very mournful.

54   *vinegar aspect*   sour looks.

56   *Nestor*   Greek hero who was both old and wise, i.e. a very serious person.
     jest   joke.

61   *prevented me*   anticipated me, beaten me to it.

62   *Your worth...regard*   I value you.

64   *embrace th'occasion*   seize the opportunity.

67   *grow exceeding strange*   have almost become strangers.

68   *We'll make...yours*   we shall be free (to meet) when it suits you.

Because you are not merry; and 't were as easy
For you to laugh and leap, and say you are merry,
Because you are not sad. Now, by two-headed
  Janus,   50
Nature hath framed strange fellows in her time;
Some that will evermore peep through their eyes,
And laugh like parrots at a bagpiper;
And other of such vinegar aspect
That they'll not show their teeth in way of smile,   55
Though Nestor swear the jest be laughable.

Enter BASSANIO, LORENZO, *and* GRATIANO.

Here comes Bassanio, your most noble kinsman,
Gratiano, and Lorenzo. Fare ye well,
We leave you now with better company.

SALERIO

I would have stayed till I had made you merry,   60
If worthier friends had not prevented me.

ANTONIO

Your worth is very dear in my regard.
I take it your own business calls on you,
And you embrace th' occasion to depart.

SALERIO

Good morrow, my good lords.   65

BASSANIO

Good signiors both, when shall we laugh? say,
  when?
You grow exceeding strange; must it be so?

SALERIO

We'll make our leisures to attend on yours.

Exeunt SALERIO *and* SOLANIO

74–5 *You have too much...care* you worry too much and this takes the pleasure out of life.

80 *mirth* enjoyment.

81–2 *my liver...groans* Gratiano is saying that he wants to enjoy himself rather than to refuse pleasure.

82 *mortifying* self-denying.

84 *grandsire* old man.

alabaster type of rock often used to make statues for tombs.

85 *jaundice* illness which causes depression, but also an embittered state of mind.

86 *peevish* discontented.

88 *visages* faces.

89 *cream and mantle* scum over (like stagnant water).

90 *wilful stillness entertain* deliberately keep quiet.

91–2 *With purpose...conceit* with the intention of gaining a reputation for being serious and wise.

93 *Sir Oracle* the voice of wisdom.

94 *ope* open.

LORENZO

My Lord Bassanio, since you have found Antonio,
We two will leave you, but at dinner-time   70
I pray you have in mind where we must meet.

BASSANIO

I will not fail you.

GRATIANO

You look not well, Signior Antonio,
You have too much respect upon the world.
They lose it that do buy it with much care –   75
Believe me, you are marvellously changed.

ANTONIO

I hold the world but as the world, Gratiano,
A stage, where every man must play a part,
And mine a sad one.

GRATIANO

              Let me play the fool;
With mirth and laughter let old wrinkles come,   80
And let my liver rather heat with wine
Than my heart cool with mortifying groans.
Why should a man whose blood is warm within
Sit like his grandsire, cut in alabaster?
Sleep when he wakes? and creep into the jaundice 85
By being peevish? I tell thee what, Antonio,
(I love thee, and 't is my love that speaks):
There are a sort of men whose visages
Do cream and mantle like a standing pond,
And do a wilful stillness entertain,   90
With purpose to be dressed in an opinion
Of wisdom, gravity, profound conceit,
As who should say, "I am Sir Oracle,
And when I ope my lips, let no dog bark."

96 *reputed*   said to be.

98–100 *If they should...fools*   according to the Gospel of Saint Matthew, any man who called another man a fool risked being sent to Hell (St Matthew 5:22).

101 *melancholy*   sad.

102 *this fool gudgeon*   small fish. Gratiano is suggesting that Antonio might be trying to gain a reputation for wisdom, but that such a reputation is really worthless.

104 *exhortation*   advice given in the form of a speech.

106 *dumb wise men*   wise person who does not speak.

108 *moe*   more.

110 *for this gear*   if this continues.

111–12 *silence...vendible*   silence is only praiseworthy in an ox tongue (dried and ready to be eaten); and in an old maid.

113 *Is that anything now?*   was all that worth listening to?

116 *bushels*   unit of measurement.

chaff   husks left after the corn has been threshed.

O my Antonio, I do know of these   95
That therefore only are reputed wise
For saying nothing; when I am very sure,
If they should speak, would almost damn those ears
Which, hearing them, would call their brothers
    fools –
I'll tell thee more of this another time.   100
But fish not with this melancholy bait
For this fool gudgeon, this opinion.
Come, good Lorenzo, (*To the others*) – fare ye well a
    while,
I'll end my exhortation after dinner.

LORENZO

Well, we will leave you then till dinner-time.   105
I must be one of these same dumb wise men,
For Gratiano never lets me speak.

GRATIANO

Well, keep me company but two years moe,
Thou shalt not know the sound of thine own tongue.

ANTONIO

Fare you well; I'll grow a talker for this gear.   110

GRATIANO

Thanks i' faith, for silence is only commendable
In a neat's tongue dried, and a maid not vendible.

                              Exeunt GRATIANO *and* LORENZO

ANTONIO

Is that anything now?

BASSANIO

Gratiano speaks an infinite deal of nothing – more
than any man in all Venice; his reasons are as two 115
grains of wheat hid in two bushels of chaff: you shall

117 *ere* before.

119 *what lady is the same* who the lady is.

123 *disabled* crippled.

124–5 *something showing...continuance* by living a grander lifestyle than I could really afford.

126–7 *Nor do I...rate* I'm not complaining about no longer being able to live like that.

128 *fairly* with honour.

129–30 *Wherein my time...gag'd* which my extravagant spending has left me bound to pay.

132 *have a warranty* have a right.

137 *the eye* sight. Antonio is saying that if the plan is as honourable as Bassanio himself then he will, of course, help.

138 *my extremest means* anything I have.

140 *shaft* arrow.

141 *self-same flight* a twin to the first arrow.

142 *advisèd* careful.

143 *adventuring* chancing.

144 *proof* example.

seek all day ere you find them, and when you have
them, they are not worth the search.

ANTONIO

    Well, tell me now what lady is the same
    To whom you swore a secret pilgrimage,   120
    That you to-day promised to tell me of.

BASSANIO

    'T is not unknown to you, Antonio,
    How much I have disabled mine estate
    By something showing a more swelling port
    Than my faint means would grant continuance;   125
    Nor do I now make moan to be abridged
    From such a noble rate, but my chief care
    Is to come fairly off from the great debts
    Wherein my time, something too prodigal,
    Hath left me gag'd. To you Antonio   130
    I owe the most in money and in love,
    And from your love I have a warranty
    To unburden all my plots and purposes
    How to get clear of all the debts I owe.

ANTONIO

    I pray you, good Bassanio, let me know it,   135
    And if it stand, as you yourself still do,
    Within the eye of honour, be assured
    My purse, my person, my extremest means
    Lie all unlocked to your occasions.

BASSANIO

    In my school-days, when I had lost one shaft,   140
    I shot his fellow of the self-same flight
    The self-same way, with more advisèd watch,
    To find the other forth, and by adventuring both,
    I oft found both; I urge this childhood proof

145 *pure innocence*   entirely honourable.

146 *wilful youth*   foolish boy.

150 *As I will*   that I will.

150–1 *or...Or*   either...or.

151–2 *or bring...first*   or bring back your second loan and remain gratefully in your debt for the first.

153–4 *herein spend...circumstance*   you are wasting time by using such a roundabout argument.

156 *making question of my uttermost*   doubting that I would spend everything.

158 *but*   only.

160 *prest unto it*   willing to do it.

165–6 *nothing...Portia*   this other Portia was married to Brutus, one of Julius Caesar's assassins, and had great strength of character.

169 *Renownèd suitors*   important men who want to marry Portia.

sunny locks   blonde hair.

170 *golden fleece*   Jason and his friends, the Argonauts, travelled to Colchis to find the golden fleece, a prize that would enable Jason to win back his kingdom.

Because what follows is pure innocence.   145
I owe you much, and, like a wilful youth,
That which I owe is lost, but if you please
To shoot another arrow that self way
Which you did shoot the first, I do not doubt,
As I will watch the aim, or to find both,   150
Or bring your latter hazard back again,
And thankfully rest debtor for the first.

ANTONIO

You know me well, and herein spend but time
To wind about my love with circumstance,
And out of doubt you do me now more wrong   155
In making question of my uttermost
Than if you had made waste of all I have.
Then do but say to me what I should do
That in your knowledge may by me be done,
And I am prest unto it: therefore speak.   160

BASSANIO

In Belmont is a lady richly left,
And she is fair, and, fairer than that word,
Of wondrous virtues. Sometimes from her eyes
I did receive fair speechless messages.
Her name is Portia, nothing undervalued   165
To Cato's daughter, Brutus' Portia,
Nor is the wide world ignorant of her worth,
For the four winds blow in from every coast
Renownèd suitors, and her sunny locks
Hang on her temples like a golden fleece,   170
Which makes her seat of Belmont Colchos' strand,
And many Jasons come in quest of her.
O my Antonio, had I but the means
To hold a rival place with one of them,

175 *I have a mind...thrift*   I have a strong feeling that I will be lucky.

176 *questionless*   without doubt.

178 *commodity*   anything to sell.

179 *a present sum*   money available right now.

180–1 *Try what...uttermost*   see how much you can borrow using my name as security; stretch my credit to its limits.

182 *furnish*   supply your needs.

183 *presently*   at once.

184–5 *and I...my sake*   I will not hesitate to borrow money either as a business deal or from friends.

1 *By my troth*   by my faith – a mild swear word.

4 *abundance*   plentiful amount.

5 *aught*   anything.

  surfeit   over-indulge.

6–7 *it is no...in the mean*   it is not a bad thing not to have too much.

8 *superfluity*   over-indulgence.

  comes sooner by   gets (white hairs) more quickly.

9 *competency*   having just enough.

I have a mind presages me such thrift   175
That I should questionless be fortunate.

ANTONIO

Thou know'st that all my fortunes are at sea,
Neither have I money, nor commodity
To raise a present sum; therefore go forth;
Try what my credit can in Venice do,   180
That shall be racked even to the uttermost
To furnish thee to Belmont to fair Portia.
Go, presently inquire, and so will I,
Where money is; and I no question make
To have it of my trust, or for my sake.   185

Exeunt

Scene two

Belmont. A room in Portia's house.

Enter PORTIA *with her waiting-woman* NERISSA.

PORTIA

By my troth, Nerissa, my little body is aweary of
this great world.

NERISSA

You would be, sweet madam, if your miseries were
in the same abundance as your good fortunes are;
and yet for aught I see, they are as sick that surfeit   5
with too much, as they that starve with nothing; it is
no mean happiness therefore to be seated in the
mean – superfluity comes sooner by white hairs, but
competency lives longer.

12–13 *If to do...good to do*   if it were as easy to do good as to know what is good.

14 *divine*   priest.

18–20 *a hot temper...the cripple*   strong emotions tend to ignore commonsense in much the same way that young people (the hare) ignore (jumps over) sensible ideas (the net).

21 *not in the fashion*   not likely.

24 *curbed*   held back.

28 *inspirations*   ideas.

30 *whereof*   where.

chooses his meaning   works out his (Portia's father's) riddle.

33 *what warmth...affection*   how do you feel.

35 *over-name them*   list them.

PORTIA

Good sentences, and well pronounced.   10

NERISSA

They would be better if well followed.

PORTIA

If to do were as easy as to know what were good to
do, chapels had been churches, and poor men's cot-
tages princes' palaces. It is a good divine that follows
his own instructions. I can easier teach twenty what   15
were good to be done than be one of the twenty to
follow mine own teaching; the brain may devise
laws for the blood, but a hot temper leaps o'er a cold
decree; – such a hare is madness the youth, to skip
o'er the meshes of good counsel the cripple. But this   20
reasoning is not in the fashion to choose me a husband. – O me, the word "choose"! I may neither
choose who I would, nor refuse who I dislike, so is
the will of a living daughter curbed by the will of a
dead father. Is it not hard, Nerissa, that I cannot   25
choose one, nor refuse none?

NERISSA

Your father was ever virtuous, and holy men at
their death have good inspirations; therefore the lottery that he hath devised in these three chests, of
gold, silver, and lead, whereof who chooses his   30
meaning chooses you, will no doubt never be chosen
by any rightly, but one who you shall rightly love.
But what warmth is there in your affection towards
any of these princely suitors that are already come?

PORTIA

I pray thee over-name them, and as thou namest   35

37 *level at* work out.

38 *Neapolitan* from Naples.

39 *colt* young male horse (it may also mean a boy).

40–1 *a great...parts* great pride in counting among his skills the fact (that he can shoe a horse himself).

42 *played false* had an affair with.

43 *smith* blacksmith.

44 *County Palatine* The Count of Palatine.

45 *as who should say* as much as to say.

an if.

47 *weeping philosopher* an ancient Greek (Heraclitus) famous for the sadness that the foolish behaviour of men caused him.

48 *unmannerly* unsuitable.

50 *death's-head...mouth* skull and crossbones.

52 *How say you by* what have you to say about?

57 *throstle* thrush.

58 *a-capering* dancing.

ACT ONE SCENE TWO

them, I will describe them. And according to my
description level at my affection.

NERISSA

First there is the Neapolitan prince.

PORTIA

Ay, that's a colt indeed, for he doth nothing but talk
of his horse, and he makes it a great appropriation 40
to his own good parts that he can shoe him himself.
I am much afeared my lady his mother played false
with a smith.

NERISSA

Then is there the County Palatine.

PORTIA

He doth nothing but frown, as who should say, "an 45
you will not have me, choose". He hears merry tales
and smiles not; I fear he will prove the weeping philosopher when he grows old, being so full of unmannerly sadness in his youth. I had rather be married
to a death's-head with a bone in his mouth, than to 50
either of these. God defend me from these two.

NERISSA

How say you by the French lord, Monsieur Le Bon?

PORTIA

God made him, and therefore let him pass for a
man. In truth I know it is a sin to be a mocker, but
he! why he hath a horse better than the Neapoli- 55
tan's, a better bad habit of frowning than the Count
Palatine; he is every man in no man; if a throstle
sing, he falls straight a-capering. He will fence with
his own shadow. If I should marry him, I should
marry twenty husbands. If he would despise me, I 60

62 *requite him*   love him as he loves me.

66 *hath neither*   does not speak either.

68 *have a poor pennyworth*   have very little.

69 *proper man's picture*   looks like a real man.

70 *dumb-show*   mime.

suited   dressed.

71 *doublet*   close fitting jacket.

round hose   tight trousers.

75 *neighbourly charity*   neighbourly concern. Portia is being sarcastic as there was a lot of bad feeling between England and Scotland at this point in history.

76 *borrowed...of the Englishman*   the Englishman boxed the Scottish lord's ear.

78–9 *became his surety...another*   became his guarantor and promised to add a blow of his own. France and England were also old enemies.

would forgive him, for if he love me to madness, I
shall never requite him.

NERISSA

What say you then to Falconbridge, the young
baron of England?

PORTIA

You know I say nothing to him, for he understands 65
not me, nor I him; he hath neither Latin, French,
nor Italian, and you will come into the court and
swear that I have a poor pennyworth in the English.
He is a proper man's picture, but alas! who can converse with a dumb-show? How oddly he is suited! I 70
think he bought his doublet in Italy, his round hose
in France, his bonnet in Germany, and his behaviour everywhere.

NERISSA

What think you of the Scottish lord, his neighbour?

PORTIA

That he hath a neighbourly charity in him, for he 75
borrowed a box of the ear of the Englishman, and
swore he would pay him again when he was able. I
think the Frenchman became his surety, and sealed
under for another.

NERISSA

How like you the young German, the Duke of Sax- 80
ony's nephew?

PORTIA

Very vilely in the morning when he is sober, and
mostly vilely in the afternoon when he is drunk;
when he is best, he is a little worse than a man, and

85 *An the worst...fell*   if the worst happens.
86 *make shift*   manage.
92 *Rhenish wine*   wine from the Rhineland of Germany.
contrary   wrong.
95 *ere*   before.
sponge   alcoholic, i.e. a man who soaks up drink like a sponge.
97–8 *acquainted me...determinations*   told me of their decision.
99 *suit*   wooing.
some other sort...imposition   some way other than by your father's scheme.
102 *Sibylla*   a wise woman who had an unnaturally long life.
103 *Diana*   Roman goddess of the moon, famous for her beauty and her virginity.
104 *parcel*   bunch.
106 *dote on*   wish for.
108 *in your father's time*   when your father was alive.
109 *hither*   here.

when he is worst he is little better than a beast. An 85
the worst fall that ever fell, I hope I shall make shift
to go without him.

NERISSA

If he should offer to choose, and choose the right
casket, you should refuse to perform your father's
will, if you should refuse to accept him. 90

PORTIA

Therefore, for fear of the worst, I pray thee set a
deep glass of Rhenish wine on the contrary casket,
for if the devil be within, and that temptation without, I know he will choose it. I will do anything,
Nerissa, ere I will be married to a sponge. 95

NERISSA

You need not fear, lady, the having any of these
lords; they have acquainted me with their deter-
minations, which it, indeed, to return to their home,
and to trouble you with no more suit, unless you
may be won by some other sort than your father's 100
imposition, depending on the caskets.

PORTIA

If I live to be as old as Sibylla, I will die as chaste as
Diana, unless I be obtained by the manner of my
father's will. I am glad this parcel of wooers are so
reasonable, for there is not one among them but I 105
dote on his very absence; and I pray God grant
them a fair departure.

NERISSA

Do you not remember, lady, in your father's time, a
Venetian, a scholar and a soldier, that came hither
in company of the Marquis of Montferrat? 110

118 *forerunner*   messenger sent on ahead.

123–5 *he have...devil*   if he is a saintly man and has a dark skin, I would rather he behaved like a priest towards me and hear me confess my sins (shrive me), than marry me.

126 *Sirrah*   way of addressing servants.

PORTIA

Yes, yes, it was Bassanio, as I think so was he called.

NERISSA

True, madam, he of all the men that ever my foolish
eyes looked upon was the best deserving a fair lady.

PORTIA

I remember him well, and I remember him worthy
of thy praise.   115

Enter a SERVING-MAN.

How now, what news?

SERVING-MAN

The four strangers seek for you, madam, to take
their leave; and there is a forerunner come from a
fifth, the Prince of Morocco, who brings word the
prince his master will be here to-night.   120

PORTIA

If I could bid the fifth welcome with so good heart
as I can bid the other four farewell, I should be glad
of his approach; if he have the condition of a saint
and the complexion of a devil, I had rather he
should shrive me than wive me.   125
Come, Nerissa. (*To the Serving-man*) Sirrah, go be-
    fore.
Whiles we shut the gate upon one wooer, another
    knocks at the door.

                                                            Exeunt

1 *ducat*   gold coin.
4 *be bound*   be responsible for paying back (the loan).
6 *stead me*   help me.
12 *imputation*   vicious rumour.

Scene three

Venice. A street.

Enter BASSANIO *with* SHYLOCK *the Jew.*

SHYLOCK
Three thousand ducats, well.

BASSANIO
Ay sir, for three months.

SHYLOCK
For three months, – well.

BASSANIO
For the which, as I told you, Antonio shall be bound.

SHYLOCK
Antonio shall become bound, – well.   5

BASSANIO
May you stead me? Will you pleasure me? Shall I
know your answer?

SHYLOCK
Three thousand ducats for three months, and Antonio bound.

BASSANIO
Your answer to that?   10

SHYLOCK
Antonio is a good man.

BASSANIO
Have you heard any imputation to the contrary?

15 *sufficient*   has enough money to guarantee.

his means are in supposition   his money is tied up in uncertain business ventures.

17 *the Rialto*   meeting place where Venetian gentlemen and merchants did business.

19 *squandered*   scattered – perhaps unwisely.

23 *notwithstanding*   despite this.

25 *bond*   legal agreement.

26 *assured*   certain.

27 *I may be assured*   Shylock is using the word 'assured' in its second, legal, sense here. He means that before he accepts the bargain he will reassure himself that it is a wise business deal.

28 *bethink me*   think carefully.

30 *pork*   there are a number of foods that Jews are not allowed to eat for religious reasons. Pork is one of these foods.

habitation   place to live in.

31 *the Nazarite*   Jesus (of Nazareth). For the full story see St Matthew 8: 28–34.

SHYLOCK

Ho no, no, no, no; my meaning in saying he is a
good man is to have you understand me that he is
sufficient. Yet his means are in supposition; he hath 15
an argosy bound to Tripolis, another to the Indies. I
understand, moreover, upon the Rialto, he hath a
third at Mexico, a fourth for England, and other
ventures he hath squandered abroad. But ships are
but boards, sailors but men; there be land-rats and 20
water-rats, water-thieves, and land-thieves, (I mean
pirates), and then there is the peril of waters, winds,
and rocks; the man is, notwithstanding, sufficient, –
three thousand ducats, – I think I may take his
bond.   25

BASSANIO

Be assured you may.

SHYLOCK

I *will* be assured I may: and, that I may be assured,
I will bethink me. May I speak with Antonio?

BASSANIO

If it please you to dine with us.

SHYLOCK

Yes, to smell pork, to eat of the habitation which 30
your prophet the Nazarite conjured the devil into. I
will buy with you, sell with you, talk with you, walk
with you, and so following, but I will not eat with
you, drink with you, nor pray with you. What news
on the Rialto? – Who is he comes here?   35

Enter ANTONIO.

BASSANIO

This is Signior Antonio.

37 *fawning*   to fawn is to flatter someone; to 'creep' because you want something.

publican   term of abuse. Publicans were the people who collected taxes for the Romans in Jesus' time. They were regarded as traitors by the Jews.

39 *low simplicity*   naively. Shylock is suggesting, perhaps sarcastically, that Antonio has no business sense.

40 *gratis*   (Latin) free, without charging interest.

41 *usance*   the rate of interest charged by the moneylenders.

42 *catch him...hip*   a hold used in wrestling matches. Shylock sees himself engaged in a struggle with Antonio.

43 *feed fat*   satisfy.

44 *sacred nation*   the Jewish people.

rails   uses bitter or abusive language.

45 *congregate*   gather

46 *thrift*   wise management of money.

47 *Which he calls interest*   Shylock prefers the term thrift for the money that he earns and is angry that Antonio refers to it as interest.

49 *debating of my present store*   trying to work out how much money I have.

51 *gross*   total amount of money.

54 *but soft*   wait a moment.

55 *Rest you fair*   I hope you are well.

56 *Your worship...mouths*   we were just talking about you.

57 *albeit*   although

58 *excess*   interest.

59 *ripe wants*   pressing needs.

60–1 *Is he yet ... ye would?*   does he know how much you need to borrow?

SHYLOCK (*Aside*)
How like a fawning publican he looks!
I hate him for he is a Christian:
But more, for that in low simplicity
He lends out money gratis, and brings down   40
The rate of usance here with us in Venice.
If I can catch him once upon the hip,
I will feed fat the ancient grudge I bear him.
He hates our sacred nation, and he rails,
Even there where merchants most do congregate,   45
On me, my bargains, and my well-won thrift,
Which he calls interest; cursed be my tribe
If I forgive him!

BASSANIO
                    Shylock, do you hear?

SHYLOCK
I am debating of my present store,
And by the near guess of my memory   50
I cannot instantly raise up the gross
Of full three thousand ducats: what of that?
Tubal, a wealthy Hebrew of my tribe,
Will furnish me; but soft! how many months
Do you desire? (*To* ANTONIO) Rest you fair, good
    signior;   55
Your worship was the last man in our mouths.

ANTONIO
Shylock, albeit I neither lend nor borrow
By taking nor by giving of excess,
Yet to supply the ripe wants of my friend,
I'll break a custom. (*To* BASSANIO) Is he yet possessed 60
How much ye would?

65 *Me thoughts*   I thought.

66 *Upon advantage*   in order to make a profit.

67 *Jacob...Laban*   see Genesis 30: 25–43 for this story. Shylock is using it to claim that he has biblical authority for charging interest. In other words, if God did not mind Jacob making a profit, why should he object to the moneylenders doing the same thing?

69 *wrought in his behalf*   worked for his benefit.

70 *possessor*   Jacob was Abraham's grandson, therefore the third in the family line to own Abraham's property.

73 *mark*   note.

74 *compromised*   agreed.

75 *eanlings*   newborn lambs.

   streaked and pied   black and white.

76 *ewes*   female sheep.

   rank   in season, ready to breed.

78 *work of generation*   mating.

80 *pilled me certain wands*   took sticks from various trees and peeled the bark off them.

81 *deed of kind*   mating.

82 *fulsome*   fertile.

SHYLOCK

           Ay, ay, three thousand ducats.

ANTONIO

  And for three months.

SHYLOCK

  I had forgot – three months; (*To* BASSANIO) you told
    me so.
  Well then, your bond; and let me see – but hear you,
  Me thoughts you said you neither lend nor borrow 65
  Upon advantage.

ANTONIO

          I do never use it.

SHYLOCK

  When Jacob grazed his uncle Laban's sheep –
  This Jacob from our holy Abram was
  (As his wise mother wrought in his behalf)
  The third possessor; ay, he was the third ...   70

ANTONIO

  And what of him? did *he* take interest?

SHYLOCK

  No, not take interest, not as you would say
  Directly interest; mark what Jacob did:
  When Laban and himself were compromised
  That all the eanlings which were streaked and pied 75
  Should fall as Jacob's hire, the ewes being rank
  In end of autumn turnèd to the rams,
  And when the work of generation was
  Between these woolly breeders in the act,
  The skilful shepherd pilled me certain wands,   80
  And in the doing of the deed of kind
  He stuck them up before the fulsome ewes,

83   *eaning*   lambing.

85   *thrive*   do well (by gaining property). By using the word 'thrive' in one line and then replacing it with the word 'thrift' in the next line, Shylock is suggesting that this biblical story shows approval for those who gain at others' expense, i.e. charge interest.

87   *served for*   served God by doing.

89   *swayed and fashioned*   carried out and thought up.

90   *inserted*   mentioned.

92   *make it breed as fast*   help it to reproduce as quickly. He is comparing his money to Jacob's ewes and rams.

94   *cite Scripture*   quote from the Bible.

95–6   *An evil soul...smiling cheek*   some evil person who can recite Scripture to make his point is as bad as a criminal who smiles as he commits his crime.

101   *beholding*   in debt.

103   *rated me*   criticised me.

104   *moneys*   term used to mean either sums of money or just money in general.

Who, then conceiving, did in eaning time
Fall parti-coloured lambs, and those were Jacob's.
This was a way to thrive, and he was blest;   85
And thrift is blessing if men steal it not.

ANTONIO

This was a venture, sir, that Jacob served for,
A thing not in his power to bring to pass,
But swayed and fashioned by the hand of heaven.
Was this inserted to make interest good?   90
Or is your gold and silver ewes and rams?

SHYLOCK

I cannot tell, I make it breed as fast –
But note me, signior ...

ANTONIO

                              Mark you this, Bassanio,
The devil can cite Scripture for his purpose;
An evil soul producing holy witness   95
Is like a villain with a smiling cheek,
A goodly apple rotten at the heart.
O what a goodly outside falsehood hath!

SHYLOCK

Three thousand ducats, 't is a good round sum.
Three months from twelve—then let me see the
    rate.   100

ANTONIO

Well, Shylock, shall we be beholding to you?

SHYLOCK

Signior Antonio, many a time and oft
In the Rialto you have rated me
About my moneys and my usances.
Still have I borne it with a patient shrug,   105

106 *sufferance*   suffering. Throughout history the Jews have often been singled out for persecution; sometimes being made to wear special tokens to set them apart from other people. The yellow star sewn onto the clothes of Jews in the Nazi concentration camps was one such badge.

107 *misbeliever*   unbeliever, not a Christian.

108 *gaberdine*   a long robe worn over other clothes.

109 *for use of*   because of.

111 *Go to*   and now look!

113 *void your rheum*   spat.

114 *foot me*   kick me.

    spurn   reject, kick.

    cur   stray dog.

115 *threshold*   legal boundary of a property.

    suit   what you are asking for.

119 *bondman's key*   very humble tone of voice suitable for a man who is owned by another man.

120 *bated breath*   humbled or lowered in speech.

129–30 *when did friendship...friend?*   when did one friend ever make money out of another friend?

132 *if he break*   fails to pay the money back.

    With better face...penalty   save your reputation and enjoy making him pay the penalty.

For sufferance is the badge of all our tribe.
You call me misbeliever, cut-throat dog,
And spit upon my Jewish gaberdine,
And all for use of that which is mine own.
Well then, it now appears you need my help.   110
Go to, then, you come to me, and you say,
"Shylock, we would have moneys"; *you* say so;
You that did void your rheum upon my beard,
And foot me as you spurn a stanger cur
Over your threshold; moneys is your suit.   115
What should I say to you? Should I not say:
"Hath a dog money? Is it possible
A cur can lend three thousand ducats?"; or
Shall I bend low, and in a bondman's key,
With bated breath and whispering humbleness   120
Say this:
"Fair sir, you spat on me on Wednesday last;
You spurned me such a day; another time
You called me dog; and for these courtesies
I'll lend you thus much moneys"?   125

ANTONIO

I am as like to call thee so again,
To spit on thee again, to spurn thee too.
If thou wilt lend this money, lend it not
As to thy friends, for when did friendship take
A breed for barren metal of his friend?   130
But lend it rather to thine enemy,
Who if he break, thou may'st with better face
Exact the penalty.

SHYLOCK
                    Why, look you, how you storm!
I would be friends with you, and have your love,
Forget the shames that you have stained me with, 135

43

136–7 *no doit...usance*   not a penny (or other equally worthless coin) of interest. Th doit was originally a Dutch coin.

138 *kind*   Shylock is using this in its usual sense, but also means that his offer is t natural one that any man would make.

140 *notary*   lawyer.

seal me   legal agreements were sealed with wax and a signet ring.

141 *single bond*   it seems probable that Shylock means that only Antonio needs t be involved in this agreement and that he will not have to provide backers to the loan if he cannot do so. However, at this point in the scene it could also mean an agreement with no penalties attached to it.

merry sport   a joke.

144 *forfeit*   penalty incurred if Antonio does not repay Shylock.

145 *nominated*   named.

148 *Content, in faith*   fine, that suits me.

151 *dwell in my necessity*   continue in the mess I've got myself into.

152 *forfeit it*   fail to pay.

159 *break his day*   fail to meet the deadline.

Supply your present wants, and take no doit
Of usance for my moneys, and you'll not hear me –
This is kind I offer.

BASSANIO

This were kindness.

SHYLOCK

              This kindness will I show.
Go with me to a notary; seal me there   140
Your single bond, and, in a merry sport,
If you repay me not on such a day,
I such a place, such sum or sums as are
Expressed in the condition, let the forfeit
Be nominated for an equal pound   145
Of your fair flesh, to be cut off and taken
In what part of your body pleaseth me.

ANTONIO

Content, in faith; I'll seal to such a bond,
And say there is much kindness in the Jew.

BASSANIO

You shall not seal to such a bond for me;   150
I'll rather dwell in my necessity.

ANTONIO

Why, fear not, man, I will not forfeit it –
Within these two months, that's a month before
This bond expires, I do expect return
Of thrice three times the value of this bond.   155

SHYLOCK

O father Abram, what these Christians are,
Whose own hard dealings teaches them suspect
The thoughts of others! Pray you, tell me this:
If he should break his day, what should I gain

160 *exaction of the forfeiture* insisting on carrying out the penalty.

162 *estimable* admirable.

165 *adieu* goodbye.

169 *direction* instructions.

170 *purse the ducats straight* collect the money (in a purse) immediately.

171 *fearful guard* unreliable guard.

172 *unthrifty* careless. Note the use of the word 'thrift' again.

knave ruffian.

173 *Hie thee* hurry yourself. Antonio is not sorry to see Shylock go!

174 *The Hebrew...grows kind* Antonio suggests that kindness is a Christian virtue, not known of in Jews. Thus Shylock is becoming a Christian. See also note to Act 1, scene 3, line 106.

175 *fair terms* a reasonable agreement.

I like not...mind Bassanio does not trust Shylock's kindness.

By the exaction of the forfeiture?   160
A pound of man's flesh taken from a man
Is not so estimable, profitable neither,
As flesh of muttons, beefs, or goats. I say,
To buy his favour I extend this friendship;
If he will take it, so; if not, adieu,   165
And for my love I pray you wrong me not.

ANTONIO

Yes, Shylock, I will seal unto this bond.

SHYLOCK

Then meet me forthwith at the notary's.
Give him direction for this merry bond,
And I will go and purse the ducats straight,   170
See to my house, left in the fearful guard
Of an unthrifty knave; and presently
I'll be with you.

Exit

ANTONIO

             Hie thee, gentle Jew.
(*To* BASSANIO) The Hebrew will turn Christian, he
   grows kind.

BASSANIO

I like not fair terms and a villain's mind.   175

ANTONIO

Come on, in this there can be no dismay;
My ships come home a month before the day.

Exeunt

47

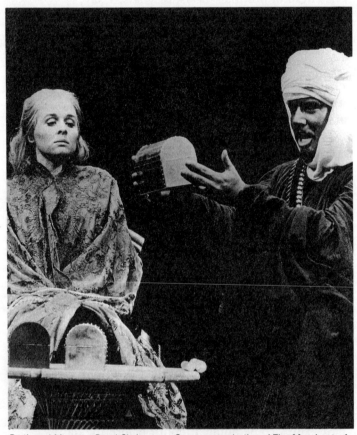

Portia and Morocco: Royal Shakespeare Company production of The Merchant of Venice, 1981.

Act 2: summary

In this Act Shylock is deserted by the only two members of his household. His servant Launcelot Gobbo (the clown of the play) decides that he would rather work for Bassanio; and his daughter Jessica elopes with her Christian lover Lorenzo (one of Bassanio's friends). When Jessica runs away she takes with her much of Shylock's hoard of money and jewels. He is furious and, as a result of this theft, greets the rumour that one of Antonio's ships has been wrecked with savage delight.

In Belmont Portia has stood by and watched both the Prince of Morocco and the Prince of Arragon face the test of the caskets. Morocco chose the gold chest, and Arragon chose the silver, neither of which contain the portrait of Portia. As the Act ends, news of Bassanio's arrival is brought to Portia.

tawny   yellowy-brown in colour.

1   *Mislike*   dislike.

2   *shadowed livery*   the dark uniform. The prince talks as if he were a servant in the Sun's household.

burnished   shiny.

5   *Phoebus*   the Sun god, traditionally pictured as riding in a chariot pulled by firey horses.

6   *incision*   a cut; both a test of bravery and a means of showing that the prince's blood is the same colour as any other man's.

8   *aspect of mine*   my appearance.

9   *feared the valiant*   frightened the bravest.

10   *best-regarded*   those seen as being the most beautiful.

11   *clime*   climate, and so by implication, country.

hue   colour.

13–14   *I am not...eyes*   I am not only influenced by finding someone attractive to look at.

15   *lottery of my destiny*   the test that will settle my future.

16   *Bars me...choosing*   prevents me choosing who I want.

17   *scanted me*   restricted me.

18   *hedged me by his wit*   in his wisdom has confined me.

yield   give up freely.

20   *renownèd*   famous.

stood as fair   has as much chance. This is also a play on the word 'fair' as the prince has a dark complexion.

Act Two

Scene one

Belmont. A room in Portia's house.

A flourish of cornets. Enter the Prince of MOROCCO, *a tawny Moor, all in white, and three or four followers accordingly, with* PORTIA, NERISSA, *and their train.*

MOROCCO

    Mislike me not for my complexion,
    The shadowed livery of the burnished sun,
    To whom I am a neighbour, and near bred.
    Bring me the fairest creature northward born,
    Where Phœbus' fire scarce thaws the icicles,   5
    And let us make incision for your love,
    To prove whose blood is reddest, his or mine.
    I tell thee, lady, this aspect of mine
    Hath feared the valiant; by my love I swear,
    The best-regarded virgins of our clime   10
    Have loved it too. I would not change this hue,
    Except to steal your thoughts, my gentle queen.

PORTIA

    In terms of choice I am not solely led
    By nice direction of a maiden's eyes;
    Besides, the lottery of my destiny   15
    Bars me the right of voluntary choosing;
    But if my father had not scanted me,
    And hedged me by his wit to yield myself
    His wife, who wins me by that means I told you,
    Your self, renownèd prince, then stood as fair   20
    As any comer I have looked on yet
    For my affection.

51

24 *scimitar*   sword with a curved blade.

25 *the Sophy*   the King of Persia.

25–6 *a Persian...Solyman*   Suleiman the Magnificent (1494–1566), Sultan of Turkey.

26 *three fields*   three battles.

27 *o'erstare*   outstare.

29–30 *Pluck the...prey*   these are acts of great bravery.

31 *alas the while*   expression of regret.

32 *Hercules and Lichas*   Hercules was a Greek hero famous for his strength. Lichas was his servant.

35 *Alcides*   Hercules was also called Alcides.

page   servant.

42 *be advised*   consider this.

43 *Nor will not*   I will not (speak to a lady about marriage).

44 *temple*   the church where Morocco will swear to abide by all the conditions that he has just agreed to.

45 *hazard*   guess, choice.

MOROCCO

               Even for that I thank you;
Therefore I pray you lead me to the caskets
To try my fortune. By this scimitar
That slew the Sophy, and a Persian prince   25
That won three fields of Sultan Solyman,
I would o'erstare the sternest eyes that look,
Outbrave the heart most daring on the earth,
Pluck the young sucking cubs from the she-bear,
Yea, mock the lion when he roars for prey,   30
To win thee, lady. But alas the while!
If Hercules and Lichas play at dice,
Which is the better man, the greater throw
May turn by fortune from the weaker hand;
So is Alcides beaten by his page,   35
And so may I, blind Fortune leading me,
Miss that which one unworthier may attain,
And die with grieving.

PORTIA

                  You must take your chance,
And either not attempt to choose at all,
Or swear before you choose, if you choose wrong,   40
Never to speak to lady afterward
In way of marriage; therefore be advised.

MOROCCO

Nor will not. Come, bring me unto my chance.

PORTIA

First, forward to the temple; after dinner
Your hazard shall be made.

MOROCCO

              Good fortune then,   45
To make me blest or cursed'st among men!
                  Sound of cornets. Exeunt

the clown   the comic character of the play, but this could also mean that Launcelot is a 'country bumpkin'.

1   *will serve me*   will allow me.

2   *the fiend*   the devil.

6   *take heed*   listen carefully.

10   *Fia*   go on!

13–14   *my conscience...heart*   Launcelot talks of his conscience hugging his heart for comfort, as if it lacked the courage to make a decision by itself.

17–18   *something smack...taste*   had a flavour, an unpleasant taste, i.e. was not as honest as he might have been. There is also a certain amount of sexual innuendo here.

21   *you counsel well*   you give good advice.

23   *God bless the mark*   God forgive me. A phrase used to excuse saying something that was considered improper, in this case the reference to the devil.

25   *saving your reverence*   phrase similar to 'God bless the mark' (above).

27   *incarnation*   he means incarnate, i.e. made flesh.

Scene two

Venice. A street.

Enter LAUNCELOT GOBBO, *the clown, alone.*

LAUNCELOT

Certainly, my conscience will serve me to run from
this Jew my master; the fiend is at mine elbow, and
tempts me, saying to me, "Gobbo, Launcelot Gobbo,
good Launcelot," or "good Gobbo", or "good
Launcelot Gobbo, use your legs, take the start, run   5
away." My conscience says, "No; take heed, honest
Launcelot, take heed, honest Gobbo," or, as
aforesaid, "honest Launcelot Gobbo; do not run,
scorn running with thy heels." Well, the most
courageous fiend bids me pack, "Fia!" says the   10
fiend, "away!" says the fiend, "for the heavens,
rouse up a brave mind," says the fiend, "and run."
Well, my conscience, hanging about the neck of my
heart, says very wisely to me: "My honest friend
Launcelot" – being an honest man's son, or rather   15
an honest woman's son, for indeed my father did
something smack, something grow to; he had a kind
of taste – well, my conscience says "Launcelot,
budge not!" "Budge!" says the fiend. "Budge not!"
says my conscience. "Conscience," say I, "you   20
counsel well; fiend," say I, "you counsel well"; to be
ruled by my conscience, I should stay with the Jew
my master, who (God bless the mark) is a kind of
devil; and to run away from the Jew I should be
ruled by the fiend, who (saving your reverence) is   25
the devil himself; certainly the Jew is the very devil
incarnation, and in my conscience, my conscience is

34 *true-begotten* begotten means 'born'. This phrase would make more sense if it had been applied by his father to Launcelot himself.

35 *sand-blind, high gravel-blind* stone-blind means completely blind, sand-blind means nearly blind, and Launcelot makes up his own phrase, 'high gravel-blind' to describe his father's eyesight.

36 *confusions* he means 'conclusions', a phrase meaning to test one's wits.

40 *marry* by the Virgin Mary; a mild swear word.

41 *turn of no hand* do not turn anywhere.

43 *By God's sonties* by God's saints; a mild swear word.

    to hit to find.

47 *now will...waters* make him cry.

but a kind of hard conscience, to offer to counsel
me to stay with the Jew; the fiend gives the more
friendly counsel: I will run, fiend; my heels are at 30
your commandment; I will run.

Enter old GOBBO *with a basket.*

GOBBO

Master young man, you I pray you, which is the
way to Master Jew's?

LAUNCELOT *(Aside)*

O heavens! this is my true-begotten father, who,
being more than sand-blind, high gravel-blind, 35
knows me not. I will try confusions with him.

GOBBO

Master young gentleman, I pray you, which is the
way to Master Jew's?

LAUNCELOT

Turn up on your right hand at the next turning, but
at the next turning of all on your left; marry, at the 40
very next turning turn of no hand, but turn down
indirectly to the Jew's house.

GOBBO

By God's sonties, 't will be a hard way to hit. Can
you tell me whether one Launcelot that dwells with
him, dwell with him or no? 45

LAUNCELOT

Talk you of young *Master* Launcelot? *(Aside)* Mark
me now, now will I raise the waters. *(To* GOBBO)
Talk you of young *Master* Launcelot?

GOBBO

No "master", sir, but a poor man's son. His father,

50 *exceeding* exceedingly, extremely.

51 *well to live* alive and well.

52 *what a will* what he will.

55 *ergo* (Latin) therefore. Launcelot is showing off.

60 *the Sisters Three* the three sisters who, according to myth, were supposed to be responsible for determining a man's fate. Launcelot is pretending to be an intellectual.

64 *the very staff of my age* my means of support, the person I rely on in my old age.

66 *cudgel* thick stick or club. Launcelot has taken the idea of a 'staff' (stick) literally!

hovel-post important structural support in a building.

68 *Alack* alas!

though I say 't, is an honest, exceeding poor man, 50
and, God be thanked, well to live.

LAUNCELOT

Well, let his father be what a will, we talk of young
Master Launcelot.

GOBBO

Your worship's friend and Launcelot, sir.

LAUNCELOT

But I pray you, ergo old man, ergo I beseech you, 55
talk you of young Master Launcelot?

GOBBO

Of Launcelot, an't please your mastership.

LAUNCELOT

Ergo Master Launcelot. Talk not of Master Launcelot, father, for the young gentleman, according to
fates and destinies, and such odd sayings, the Sis- 60
ters Three, and such branches of learning, is indeed
deceased, or, as you would say in plain terms, gone
to heaven.

GOBBO

Marry, God forbid! The boy was the very staff of my
age, my very prop. 65

LAUNCELOT (*Aside*)

Do I look like a cudgel or a hovel-post, a staff, or a
prop? – Do you know me, father?

GOBBO

Alack the day! I know you not, young gentleman,
but I pray you tell me, is my boy, God rest his soul,
alive or dead? 70

74–5 *wise father...child*   Launcelot's own version of 'it is a wise child that knows its
   own father'.

92 *beard*   his father is feeling the back of his head rather than his face.

LAUNCELOT

Do you not know me, father?

GOBBO

Alack, sir, I am sand-blind; I know you not.

LAUNCELOT

Nay indeed, if you had your eyes you might fail of
the knowing me; it is a wise father that knows his
own child. Well, old man, I will tell you news of 75
your son. (*Kneels with his back to* GOBBO) Give me
your blessing; truth will come to light, murder cannot be hid long – a man's son may, but in the end
truth will out.

GOBBO (*placing his hands on* LAUNCELOT'S *head*)
Pray you, sir, stand up; I am sure you are not Laun- 80
celot my boy.

LAUNCELOT

Pray you, let's have no more fooling about it, but give
me your blessing; I am Launcelot your boy that
was, your son that is, your child that shall be.

GOBBO

I cannot think you are my son. 85

LAUNCELOT

I know not what I shall think of that; but I am
Launcelot, the Jew's man, and I am sure Margery
your wife is my mother.

GOBBO

Her name is Margery indeed; I'll be sworn, if thou
be Launcelot, thou art mine own flesh and blood. 90
(*He feels the back of* LAUNCELOT'S *head*) Lord! (wor-
shipped might He be), what a beard hast thou got!

94 *fill-horse*   horse used for pulling carts.

95–6 *grows backward*   i.e. becomes shorter rather than growing longer.

100 *how 'gree you now?*   how do you get on (with Shylock) now?

101–2 *I have set up my rest*   I have decided.

104 *halter*   hangman's noose.

109 *rare new liveries*   wonderful new uniforms. A livery was a distinctive uniform worn by the servants of important people. Each household had its own uniform.

113–4 *be so hasted*   done so speedily.

114 *at the farthest*   at the latest.

115–6 *put the liveries to making*   order the liveries to be made.

116 *anon*   immediately.

Thou hast got more hair on thy chin than Dobbin
my fill-horse has on his tail.

LAUNCELOT

It should seem, then, that Dobbin's tail grows back- 95
ward. I am sure he had more hair of his tail than
I have of my face, when I last saw him.

GOBBO

Lord, how art thou changed! How dost thou and
thy master agree? I have brought him a present;
how 'gree you now?   100

LAUNCELOT

Well, well; but for mine own part, as I have set up
my rest to run away, so I will not rest till I have run
some ground; my master's a very Jew. Give him a
present? give him a halter! I am famished in his service. (*He makes* GOBBO *feel the fingers of his left hand,* 105
which he stretches out on his chest like ribs) You may tell
every finger I have with my ribs. Father, I am glad
you are come; give me your present to one Master
Bassanio, who indeed gives rare new liveries; if I
serve not him, I will run as far as God has any 110
ground. O rare fortune! here comes the man; to him
father, for I am a Jew if I serve the Jew any longer.

Enter BASSANIO *with* LEONARDO *and a follower or two.*

BASSANIO

(*To one of the men*) You may do so, but let it be so
hasted that supper be ready at the farthest by five of
the clock. See these letters delivered, put the liveries 115
to making, and desire Gratiano to come anon to my
lodging.

Exit the man

120 *Gramercy* God grant mercy; an expression of surprise.

aught anything.

124 *infection* he means affection, i.e. desire.

129 *scarce cater-cousins* not on friendly terms with one another.

132 *fruitify* he means testify.

135 *impertinent* he means pertinent; has to do with.

LAUNCELOT

To him, father.

GOBBO

(*To* BASSANIO) God bless your worship.

BASSANIO

Gramercy, wouldst thou aught with me?   120

GOBBO

Here's my son, sir, a poor boy –

LAUNCELOT

Not a poor boy, sir, but the rich Jew's man that
would, sir – as my father shall specify –

GOBBO

He hath a great infection, sir, (as one would say) to
serve –   125

LAUNCELOT

Indeed, the short and the long is, I serve the Jew,
and have a desire – as many father shall specify –

GOBBO

His master and he (saving your worship's reverence) are scarce cater-cousins, –

LAUNCELOT

To be brief, the very truth is that the Jew, having 130
done me wrong, doth cause me, – as my father
(being, I hope, an old man) shall frutify unto you –

GOBBO

I have here a dish of doves that I would bestow
upon your worship, and my suit is –

LAUNCELOT

In very brief, the suit is impertinent to myself, as 135

141 *defect*   he means effect, heart of the matter.

142 *obtained thy suit*   got your wish.

144 *preferred thee*   recommended you for promotion.

preferment   promotion.

147–9 *The old proverb...enough*   the proverb referred to states that God's grace provides all that is needed. See 2 Corinthians 12:9.

147 *well parted*   divided equally between.

151–2 *inquire...lodgings out*   find out where I live.

153 *More guarded*   with greater decoration, possibly to indicate that Launcelot has been hired as Bassanio's fool.

154–5 *cannot get a service...head*   Launcelot continues to turn the truth on its head. He has, of course, got 'a service' (a place) in Bassanio's household and, as he has proved only too well, he has a tongue in his head!

156 *a fairer table*   he is looking at the palm of his hand. In the rest of this speech he proceeds to read his own fortune using the life line and love line that form the basis of genuine palmistry.

your worship shall know by this honest old man –
and though I say it, though old man, yet, poor man,
my father.

BASSANIO

One speak for both! – What would you?

LAUNCELOT

Serve you, sir.   140

GOBBO

That is the very defect of the matter, sir.

BASSANIO

I know thee well; thou hast obtained thy suit,
Shylock thy master spoke with me this day,
And hath preferred thee, if it *be* preferment
To leave a rich Jew's service, to become   145
The follower of so poor a gentleman.

LAUNCELOT

The old proverb is very well parted between my
master Shylock and you, sir; you have "the grace of
God", sir, and he hath "enough".

BASSANIO

Thou speak'st it well; (*To* GOBBO) go, father, with
thy son –   150
(*To* LAUNCELOT) Take leave of thy old master, and
inquire.
My lodging out. (*To his followers*) Give him a livery
More guarded than his fellows'; see it done.

LAUNCELOT

Father, in; – I cannot get a service, no! I have ne'er
a tongue in my head. (*He looks at the palm of his hand*) 155
Well, if any man in Italy have a fairer table which

157 *doth offer...book* is prepared to swear to it on the Bible.

I shall have Launcelot means 'he' (the other man) shall have.

160 *aleven* eleven.

simple coming-in income.

161–3 *scape...featherbed* to escape drowning three times only nearly to die by falling out of bed (possibly because of the eleven wives!).

164 *good wench for this gear* a good girl having given me all this.

165 *in the twinkling* (of an eye), very quickly.

167 *orderly bestowed* put away neatly (on the ship that will take them to Belmont).

168–9 *I do feast...acquaintance* I am giving a dinner tonight for my best friend.

169 *Hie thee* hurry yourself.

170 *My best...herein* I will do my best in these matters.

172 *Yonder* over there.

doth offer to swear upon a book, I shall have good
fortune! Go to, here's a simple line of life, here's a
small trifle of wives; alas! fifteen wives is nothing,
aleven widows and nine maids is a simple coming-in 160
for one man, and then to scape drowning thrice, and
to be in peril of my life with the edge of a feather-
bed, here are simple scapes. Well, if Fortune be a
woman, she's a good wench for this gear. Father,
come; I'll take my leave of the Jew in the twinkling. 165

Exit with old GOBBO

BASSANIO
I pray thee, good Leonardo, think on this;
These things being bought and orderly bestowed,
Return in haste, for I do feast to-night
My best-esteemed acquaintance. Hie thee, go!

LEONARDO
My best endeavours shall be done herein. 170

He begins to leave.

Enter GRATIANO.

GRATIANO
Where's your master?

LEONARDO
Yonder, sir, he walks.

Exit

GRATIANO
Signior Bassanio!

BASSANIO
Gratiano!

174 *I have suit to you*   I have a favour to ask.

176 *deny me*   refuse me.

178 *too rude*   do not have good manners.

179 *Parts*   ways of behaving.

182 *too liberal*   too unrestrained.

183–4 *To allay...spirit*   to dilute your high spirits with more appropriate behaviour.

185 *misconstered*   misconstrued, judged wrongly.

187 *sober habit*   serious behaviour.

189 *demurely*   modestly, coyly.

190 *hood*   shield, hide.

192 *observance of civility*   good manners expected in polite society.

193 *ostent*   outward show.

195 *bearing*   how you conduct yourself.

GRATIANO

I have suit to you.

BASSANIO

                    You have obtained it.   175

GRATIANO

You must not deny me; I must go with you to
   Belmont.

BASSANIO

Why then you must – but hear thee, Gratiano;
Thou art too wild, too rude, and bold of voice,
Parts that become thee happily enough,
And in such eyes as ours appear not faults.   180
But where thou art not known, why, there they
   show
Something too liberal. Pray thee, take pain
To allay with some cold drops of modesty
Thy skipping spirit, lest through thy wild behaviour
I be misconstered in the place I go to,   185
And lose my hopes.

GRATIANO

                Signior Bassanio, hear me:
If I do not put on a sober habit,
Talk with respect, and swear but now and then,
Wear prayer-books in my pocket, look demurely,
Nay more, while grace is saying, hood mine eyes   190
Thus with my hat, and sigh and say "amen",
Use all the observance of civility
Like one well studied in a sad ostent
To please his grandam, never trust me more.

BASSANIO

Well, we shall see your bearing.   195

196 *bar to-night*   rule out tonight.

gauge me   judge me.

198 *entreat*   beg.

199 *boldest suit of mirth*   best display of happiness.

200 *That purpose merriment*   intend to enjoy themselves.

3 *Didst rob...tediousness*   took away some of its dullness.

GRATIANO

Nay, but I bar to-night; you shall not gauge me
By what we do to-night.

BASSANIO

                No, that were pity;
I would entreat you rather to put on
Your boldest suit of mirth, for we have friends
That purpose merriment. But fare you well;   200
I have some business.

GRATIANO

And I must to Lorenzo and the rest;
But we will visit you at supper-time.

                               Exeunt

Scene three

Venice. A street.

Enter JESSICA *and* LAUNCELOT, *the clown.*

JESSICA

I am sorry thou wilt leave my father so;
Our house is hell, and thou, a merry devil,
Didst rob it of some taste of tediousness.
But fare thee well; (*She gives him some money*) there is a
    ducat for thee,
And Launcelot, soon at supper shalt thou see   5
Lorenzo, who is thy new master's guest;
Give him this letter, do it secretly;
And so farewell; I would not have my father
See me in talk with thee.

10 *Adieu* farewell.

exhibit my tongue he means inhibit, in other words he cannot speak for tears.

11 *pagan* not a Christian, i.e. Jew.

12 *knave* cunning man.

13 *something* somewhat.

16 *heinous* hateful.

19 *to his manners* to the way in which he behaves.

20 *strife* conflict.

1 *slink* sneak away.

5 *have not spoke us* talked about.

LAUNCELOT

    Adieu! tears exhibit my tongue, most beautiful   10
pagan, most sweet Jew! if a Christian do not play
the knave and get thee, I am much deceived; but
adieu! these foolish drops do something drown my
manly spirit; adieu!

Exit

JESSICA

    Farewell, good Launcelot.   15
Alack, what heinous sin is it in me
To be ashamed to be my father's child!
But though I am a daughter to his blood
I am not to his manners. O Lorenzo,
If thou keep promise I shall end this strife,   20
Become a Christian, and thy loving wife!

Exit

Scene four

Venice. A street.

Enter GRATIANO, LORENZO, SALERIO *and* SOLANIO.

LORENZO

    Nay, we will slink away in supper-time,
Disguise us at my lodging, and return
All in an hour.

GRATIANO

    We have not made good preparation.

SALERIO

    We have not spoke us yet of torch-bearers.   5

6 *'T is...ordered*   it will go wrong unless it is carefully planned.

9 *to furnish us*   to get everything we need.

10–11 *An it...signify*   if you open it (break the seal) you will find out.

12 *the hand*   the handwriting.

16 *Whither*   where.

17 *Marry*   by the Virgin Mary; a mild swear word.

SOLANIO

'T is vile unless it may be quaintly ordered,
And better in my mind not undertook.

LORENZO

'T is now but four of clock; we have two hours
To furnish us —

Enter LAUNCELOT, *with a letter.*

                        friend Launcelot, what's the news?

LAUNCELOT

An it shall please you to break up this, it shall seem   10
to signify.

LORENZO

I know the hand; in faith, 't is a fair hand,
And whiter than the paper it writ on
Is the fair hand that writ.

GRATIANO

                        Love-news, in faith.

LAUNCELOT

By your leave, sir.   15

LORENZO

Whither goest thou?

LAUNCELOT

Marry, sir, to bid my old master the Jew to sup to-
night with my new master the Christian.

LORENZO

Hold here, take this; (*He gives* LAUNCELOT *some
money*) tell gentle Jessica
I will not fail her; speak it privately, (*Exit
LAUNCELOT*)   20

77

22 *masque*   party or ball at which masks were worn.

23 *am provided of*   have provided myself with.

24 *gone about it straight*   I'll do it straight away.

23 *hence*   from now.

30 *I must needs*   I must, I have to.

    hath directed   given instructions.

32 *furnished*   provided.

33 *What page's suit...readiness*   the suit of clothes that she will use to disguise herself as Lorenzo's pageboy or torch-bearer.

34 *e'er*   ever.

36–8 *never dare...Jew*   never let any harm be done to her, unless it occurs because she is the Jew's daughter.

39 *peruse*   read.

Go. – Gentlemen,
Will you prepare you for this masque to-night?
I am provided of a torch-bearer.

SALERIO

Ay, marry, I'll be gone about it straight.

SOLANIO

And so will I.   25

LORENZO

Meet me and Gratiano
At Gratiano's lodging some hour hence.

SALERIO

'T is good we do so.

Exeunt SALERIO *and* SOLANIO

GRATIANO

Was not that letter from fair Jessica?

LORENZO

I must needs tell thee all: she hath directed   30
How I shall take her from her father's house,
What gold and jewels she is furnished with,
What page's suit she hath in readiness.
If e'er the Jew her father come to heaven,
It will be for his gentle daughter's sake;   35
And never dare misfortune cross her foot,
Unless she do it under this excuse,
That she is issue to a faithless Jew;
Come, go with me, peruse this as thou goest.
Fair Jessica shall be my torch-bearer.   40

Exeunt

3 *gormandize* eat a lot.

5 *rend apparel out* ruin your clothes.

11 *bid forth* invited out.

12 *wherefore* why.

14–15 *to feed...Christian* to eat out at the extravagant Christian's expense.

15 *Look to* look after.

16 *right loath* very reluctant.

Scene five

Venice. In front of Shylock's House.

Enter SHYLOCK *the Jew and* LAUNCELOT *his man, who was the clown.*

SHYLOCK

Well, thou shalt see, thy eyes shall be thy judge,
The difference of old Shylock and Bassanio; –
(*He calls out*) What, Jessica! – (*To* LAUNCELOT) thou
    shalt not gormandize
As thou hast done with me – what, Jessica! –
And sleep, and snore, and rend apparel out. –   5
Why, Jessica I say!

LAUNCELOT

              Why, Jessica!

SHYLOCK

Who bids thee call? I do not bid thee call.

LAUNCELOT

Your worship was wont to tell me I could do
nothing without bidding.

Enter JESSICA.

JESSICA

Call you? what is your will?   10

SHYLOCK

I am bid forth to supper, Jessica;
There are my keys – but wherefore should I go?
I am not bid for love; they flatter me;
But yet I'll go in hate, to feed upon
The prodigal Christian. Jessica, my girl,   15
Look to my house. – I am right loath to go;

17 *some ill...rest*   some trouble looming that will disturb me.

19 *beseech*   ask, beg.

20 *reproach*   he means approach.

22 *conspired*   plotted. Launcelot is referring to the plans for the evening's entertainment.

23–7 *was not for nothing...afternoon*   another speech like Launcelot's attempt at palmistry. This time, prompted by Shylock's reference to his dream, he talks of omens and portents.

30 *wry*   deformed, twisted. This refers to the way in which the player had to hold the fife (a kind of flute) with his neck twisted sideways.

31 *casements*   windows.

33 *varnished faces*   the masks worn by people attending the masque.

33 *But stop...casements*   close the windows (the ears of the house, through which the noise on the street is heard).

35 *fopp'ry*   foolishness.

36 *sober*   serious.

Jacob's staff   the one possession that Jacob started out with before he went on to greatness. See Genesis 32:10. Shylock is swearing by a holy relic.

There is some ill a-brewing towards my rest,
For I did dream of money-bags to-night.

LAUNCELOT

I beseech you, sir, go; my young master doth expect
your reproach.   20

SHYLOCK

So do I his.

LAUNCELOT

And they have conspired together; I will not say you
shall see a masque, but if you do, then it was not for
nothing that my nose fell a-bleeding on Black-
Monday last, at six o'clock i' th' morning, falling   25
out that year on Ash-Wednesday was four year in
th' afternoon.

SHYLOCK

What, are there masques? – Hear you me, Jessica,
Lock up my doors, and when you hear the drum,
And the vile squealing of the wry-necked fife,   30
Clamber not you up to the casements then,
Nor thrust your head into the public street
To gaze on Christian fools with varnished faces;
But stop my house's ears – I mean my casements,
Let not the sound of shallow fopp'ry enter   35
My sober house. By Jacob's staff I swear
I have no mind of feasting forth to-night;
But I will go. (*To* LAUNCELOT) Go you before me,
    sirrah;
Say I will come.

LAUNCELOT

                    I will go before, sir.

42 *worth a Jewess' eye* proverbial saying that means worth a lot of money.

43 *Hagar's offspring* an insult. For the story of Hagar see Genesis 16.

45 *patch* fool. Court jesters wore patched clothing.

    huge feeder he eats a great deal.

46 *in profit* in improving himself.

47 *drones* a drone is a male bee that neither works nor produces honey.

    hive to live (in a beehive).

49–50 *To one...purse* Shylock hopes that Launcelot will help Bassanio spend the money that he has borrowed.

53 *Fast bind, fast find* if you shut something up securely then that is the way you will find it when you come back for it.

54 *stale* out of fashion.

55 *crost* crossed, opposed.

(*To* JESSICA) Mistress, look out at window, for all
    this –   40
There will come a Christian by
Will be worth a Jewess' eye.

Exit

SHYLOCK

What says that fool of Hagar's offspring? ha?

JESSICA

His words were, "Farewell, mistress"; nothing else.

SHYLOCK

The patch is kind enough, but a huge feeder,   45
Snail-slow in profit, and he sleeps by day
More than the wild-cat; drones hive not with me,
Therefore I part with him, and part with him
To one that I would have him help to waste
His borrowed purse. Well, Jessica, go in –   50
Perhaps I will return immediately –
Do as I bid you; shut doors after you –
"Fast bind, fast find" –
A proverb never stale in thrifty mind.

Exit

JESSICA

Farewell; – and if my fortune be not crost,   55
I have a father, you a daughter, lost

Exit

1 *penthouse* porch. The back of an Elizabethan stage had a roofed area with a balcony stage above it.

2 *Desired us to make stand* wanted us to wait.

3–4 *it is marvel...clock* it is strange that he is late, because usually lovers are the most impatient.

5–7 *ten times...unforfeited* the chariot of the goddess of Love (Venus) was supposed to be pulled by doves (pigeons in this passage). Salerio is saying that people who have only just fallen in love rush to keep their promises to one another, whereas they are slower to meet the demands of formal oaths. The comparison here may be between getting engaged and getting married.

8 *That ever holds* that is always the case.

10–12 *Where is the horse...first* where is the horse that would retrace his steps with the same amount of energy that he had when he set out on his journey?

14 *younger* young man of breeding.

prodigal someone who spends money freely.

15 *scarfèd bark* ship decorated with flags at the beginning of a voyage.

native bay home port.

16 *strumpet* prostitute, and therefore unfaithful.

18 *over-weathered ribs* the ship's sides that have been exposed to bad weather.

19 *rent* torn.

Scene six

The same.

Enter GRATIANO *and* SALERIO, *dressed for the masque.*

GRATIANO

This is the penthouse under which Lorenzo
Desired us to make stand.

SALERIO

His hour is almost past.

GRATIANO

And it is marvel he out-dwells his hour,
For lovers ever run before the clock.

SALERIO

O ten times faster Venus' pigeons fly   5
To seal love's bonds new-made, than they are wont
To keep obligèd faith unforfeited!

GRATIANO

That ever holds; who riseth from a feast
With that keen appetite that he sits down?
Where is the horse that doth untread again   10
His tedious measures with the unbated fire
That he did pace them first? All things that are,
Are with more spirit chasèd than enjoyed.
How like a younger or a prodigal
The scarfèd bark puts from her native bay,   15
Hugged and embracèd by the strumpet wind!
How like the prodigal doth she return
With over-weathered ribs and ragged sails,
Lean, rent, and beggared by the strumpet wind!

20 *hereafter*   later.

21 *long abode*   my lateness.

25 *dwells*   lives.

   my father   with luck Shylock will soon be Lorenzo's father-in-law.

27 *Albeit*   although.

   tongue   voice.

35 *my exchange*   disguise. It is worth noting here that in Shakespeare's time the women's roles in plays were performed by boys. Shakespeare's audience, therefore, would have doubly appreciated the following dialogue.

Enter LORENZO.

SALERIO
    Here comes Lorenzo; more of this hereafter.   20

LORENZO
    Sweet friends, your patience for my long abode;
    Not I but my affairs have made you wait;
    When you shall please to play the thieves for wives,
    I'll watch as long for you then. Approach –
    Here dwells my father Jew. Ho! who's within?   25

Enter JESSICA *above, in boy's clothes.*

JESSICA
    Who are you? – tell me, for more certainty –
    Albeit I'll swear that I do know your tongue.

LORENZO
    Lorenzo and thy love.

JESSICA
    Lorenzo, certain, and my love indeed;
    For who love I so much? and now who knows   30
    But you Lorenzo whether I am yours?

LORENZO
    Heaven and thy thoughts are witness that thou art.

JESSICA (*Throwing down a box*)
    Here, catch this casket; it is worth the pains.
    I am glad 't is night – you do not look on me –
    For I am much ashamed of my exchange;   35
    But love is blind, and lovers cannot see
    The pretty follies that themselves commit,
    For if they could, Cupid himself would blush
    To see me thus transformèd to a boy.

41 *hold...shames*   illuminate, shine light on this disguise that is causing me so much embarrassment.

42 *good sooth*   in truth.

too too light   'light' here means immodest, but there is also a pun on the light that Jessica must carry.

43–4 *'t is an office...obscured*   she means that she will draw attention to herself and this is the last thing that they should be doing.

44 *So are you*   i.e. she is obscured, disguised.

45 *garnish*   clothes.

47 *doth play the runaway*   the night is passing.

48 *stayed for*   waited for.

49–50 *gild myself...ducats*   to gild is to cover something with gold. Jessica is going to take more of Shylock's ducats.

51 *by my hood*   there seems to be no good reason why Gratiano should swear by this item of clothing.

a gentle   a kind person, but also a pun on the word Gentile, a non-Jew. This is one of many examples in the play of Jews being seen unfavourably.

52 *Beshrew me*   damn me.

57 *constant*   trustworthy, steadfast.

59 *masquing males*   companions at the party.

by this time   must now (be waiting for us).

LORENZO

Descend, for you must be my torch-bearer.   40

JESSICA

What, must I hold a candle to my shames?
They in themselves, good sooth, are too too light.
Why, 't is an office of discovery, love,
And I should be obscured.

LORENZO

                So are you, sweet,
Even in the lovely garnish of a boy.   45
But come at once,
For the close night doth play the runaway,
And we are stayed for at Bassanio's feast.

JESSICA

I will make fast the doors, and gild myself
With some more ducats, and be with you straight. 50

                              Exit

GRATIANO

Now, by my hood, a gentle and no Jew.

LORENZO

Beshrew me but I love her heartily;
For she is wise, if I can judge of her;
And fair she is, if that mine eyes be true;
And true she is, as she hath proved herself: 55
And therefore like herself, wise, fair, and true,
Shall she be placèd in my constant soul.

Enter JESSICA, *below.*

(*To* JESSICA) What, art thou come? – On, gentlemen,
    away!
Our masquing mates by this time for us stay.

62 *Fie, fie* well really! Antonio is impatient.

63 *all stay for you* are all waiting for you.

64 *is come about* is blowing in the right direction (for the ship to leave).

67 *on't* of it.

trains attendants.

1 *discover* show.

Exit with JESSICA *and* SALERIO; GRATIANO *is about to follow them.*

Enter ANTONIO.

ANTONIO
Who's there? 60

GRATIANO
Signior Antonio?

ANTONIO
Fie, fie, Gratiano! where are all the rest?
'T is nine o'clock; our friends all stay for you.
No masque to-night – the wind is come about;
Bassanio presently will go aboard; 65
I have sent twenty out to seek for you.

GRATIANO
I am glad on 't; I desire no more delight
Than to be under sail, and gone to-night.

Exeunt

Scene seven

Belmont. A room in Portia's house.

Flourish of cornets. Enter PORTIA *with* MOROCCO *and both their trains.*

PORTIA (*To her attendants*)
Go, draw aside the curtains and discover
The several caskets to this noble prince:-
(*To* MOROCCO) Now make your choice.

8 *dull...blunt*   a pun. 'Dull' can mean either not shiny or unsharp. 'Blunt', as well as its usual meaning, could mean outspoken or unworthy (base).

9 *hazard*   risk.

12 *withal*   as well.

14 *survey...again*   read the inscriptions over again.

19 *fair advantages*   a worthwhile profit.

20 *dross*   something that is worthless.

21 *I'll then...lead*   I'll neither give nor gamble anything for what might be in the lead casket.

22 *virgin hue*   a reference both to the colour of silver and also to the fact that silver was the metal associated with Diana, goddess of the moon. See note to Act 1, scene 2, line 103.

25 *even*   fair.

26 *rated by thy estimation*   judged by your own values.

27–30 *and yet...myself*   and yet to be afraid that I do not deserve that much does not reflect creditably upon myself.

MOROCCO

This first of gold, who this inscription bears:
"Who chooseth me shall gain what many men de-
 sire."   5
The second silver, which this promise carries:
"Who chooseth me shall get as much as he deserves."
This third, dull lead, with warning all as blunt,
"Who chooseth me must give and hazard all he
 hath."
How shall I know if I do choose the right?   10

PORTIA

The one of them contains my picture, prince;
If you choose that, then I am yours withal.

MOROCCO

Some god direct my judgement! let me see,
I will survey th' inscriptions back again; –
What says this leaden casket?   15
"Who chooseth me must give and hazard all he hath."
Must give – for what? for lead, hazard for lead!
This casket threatens – men that hazard all
Do it in hope of fair advantages;
A golden mind stoops not to shows of dross, 20
I'll then nor give nor hazard aught for lead.
What says the silver with her virgin hue?
"Who chooseth me shall get as much as he deserves."
As much as he deserves! – Pause there, Morocco,
And weigh thy value with an even hand; – 25
If thou be'st rated by thy estimation,
Thou dost deserve enough, and yet enough
May not extend so far as to the lady;
And yet to be afeard of my deserving
Were but a weak disabling of myself.   30
As much as I deserve! – why, that's the lady!

32 *in birth deserve her*   he is of as noble a family as hers.

35 *strayed*   wandered (in his thoughts).

36 *graved*   engraved.

39 *four corners of the earth*   the earth can be seen as having four corners on a map of that period.

40 *to kiss this shrine*   a shrine is a place associated with a particular saint. They often (especially in Shakespeare's time) contained holy relics that were kissed by pilgrims who visited the shrines.

   mortal   human. Portia is like a saint or goddess, but is human.

41 *Hyrcanian*   a desert south of the Caspian Sea, famous for its bleak terrain and the savagery of its wild animals.

   vasty   vast, immense.

42 *as throughfares*   as roads.

44–5 *whose ambitions...heaven*   the head (or top) of the sea attempts to spit at the sky. Morocco is describing a storm at sea.

45 *bar*   obstacle.

46 *foreign spirits*   people from abroad.

50 *base*   unworthy, but also a play on the fact that lead is a base (worthless) metal.

50–1 *it were...grave*   it would be too gross an idea to imagine her burial sheet (and therefore Portia herself) enclosed in lead as if she were in her grave.

52 *immured*   imprisoned, shut away.

53 *tried*   tried and tested.

56–7 *a coin...gold*   a gold coin in use in Shakespeare's time. It had a picture on it of the archangel Michael.

57 *insculped*   engraved.

60 *thrive I as I may*   let me do as well as I can.

61 *form*   portrait.

I do in birth deserve her, and in fortunes,
In graces, and in qualities of breeding;
But more than these, in love I do deserve –
What if I strayed no further, but chose here?   35
Let's see once more this saying graved in gold:
"Who chooseth me shall gain what many men
   desire";
Why, that's the lady – all the world desires her.
From the four corners of the earth they come
To kiss this shrine, this mortal breathing saint.   40
The Hyrcanian deserts, and the vasty wilds
Of wide Arabia are as throughfares now
For princes to come view fair Portia.
The watery kingdom, whose ambitious head
Spets in the face of heaven, is no bar   45
To stop the foreign spirits, but they come
As o'er a brook to see fair Portia.
One of these three contains her heavenly picture.
Is 't like that lead contains her? – 't were damnation
To think so base a thought; it were too gross   50
To rib her cerecloth in the obscure grave; –
Or shall I think in silver she's immured,
Being ten times undervalued to tried gold?
O sinful thought! never so rich a gem
Was set in worse than gold. They have in England   55
A coin that bears the figure of an angel
Stamped in gold, but that's insculped upon;
But here an angel in a golden bed
Lies all within. – Deliver me the key;
Here do I choose, and thrive I as I may!   60

PORTIA

There, take it, prince, and if my form lie there,
Then I am yours!

63 *A carrion Death*   a skull.

65 *glisters*   shines, glitters.

68 *my outside*   the gold that the casket is made of.

72 *inscrolled*   written on a scroll, a rolled up piece of paper.

73 *suit is cold*   you have failed in your attempt to gain a wife.

77 *tedious*   extended.

   part   go (home).

78 *a gentle riddance*   a polite good riddance.

79 *all of his complexion*   everyone his colour – but Portia could also mean
   everyone who behaves like he does.

He unlocks the golden casket.

MOROCCO

              O hell! what have we here?
A carrion Death, within whose empty eye
There is a written scroll; – I'll read the writing.

> *All that glisters is not gold;*   65
> *Often have you heard that told.*
> *Many a man his life hath sold*
> *But my outside to behold –*
> *Gilded tombs do worms infold;*
> *Had you been as wise as bold,*   70
> *Young in limbs, in judgement old,*
> *Your answer had not been inscrolled –*
> *Fare you well; your suit is cold.*

    Cold indeed and labour lost;
    Then, farewell, heat, and welcome, frost!   75
Portia, adieu! I have too grieved a heart
To take a tedious leave; thus losers part.

Exit with his train

PORTIA

A gentle riddance. (*To her attendants*) Draw the cur-
    tains; go; –
Let all of his complexion choose me so.

Exeunt

1 *under sail*   i.e. Bassanio's ship has set sail.

10 *certified*   testified to.

12 *passion so confused*   such a mixed outburst of anger.

13 *variable*   changeable.

15 *ducats*   gold coins.

19 *double ducats*   coins worth double the value of ordinary ducats.

Scene eight

Venice. A street.

Enter SALERIO *and* SOLANIO.

SALERIO

    Why, man, I saw Bassanio under sail;
    With him is Gratiano gone along,
    And in their ship I am sure Lorenzo is not.

SOLANIO

    The villain Jew with outcries raised the Duke,
    Who went with him to search Bassanio's ship.   5

SALERIO

    He came too late; the ship was under sail;
    But there the Duke was given to understand
    That in a gondola were seen together
    Lorenzo and his amorous Jessica.
    Besides, Antonio certified the Duke   10
    They were not with Bassanio in his ship.

SOLANIO

    I never heard a passion so confused,
    So strange, outrageous, and so variable,
    As the dog Jew did utter in the streets:
    "My daughter! O my ducats! O my daughter!   15
    Fled with a Christian! O my Christian ducats!
    Justice, the law, my ducats, and my daughter!
    A sealèd bag, two sealèd bags of ducats,
    Of double ducats, stolen from me by my daughter!
    And jewels, two stones, two rich and precious
      stones,   20
    Stolen by my daughter! Justice! find the girl!
    She hath the stones upon her, and the ducats!"

25 *look he keep his day*   make sure he meets his deadline (to pay the money back).

27 *reasoned*   spoke.

28 *the narrow seas*   the English Channel.

29 *miscarried*   was wrecked.

30 *richly fraught*   carrying valuable cargo.

37–8 *make some speed Of his return*   hasten his return, hurry back.

39 *Slubber not*   do not be careless with.

40 *stay the very riping of the time*   wait until time has proved fruitful, i.e. until you have got what you want.

44 *ostents*   outward shows.

45 *conveniently become you there*   be of most use to you there.

46 *even there*   then.

big with   full of.

SALERIO

Why all the boys in Venice follow him,
Crying, his stones, his daughter, and his ducats.

SOLANIO

Let good Antonio look he keep his day   25
Or he shall pay for this.

SALERIO

                    Marry, well remembered, –
I reasoned with a Frenchman yesterday,
Who told me, in the narrow seas that part
The French and English, there miscarried
A vessel of our country, richly fraught;   30
I thought upon Antonio when he told me,
And wished in silence that it were not his.

SOLANIO

You were best to tell Antonio what you hear;
Yet do not suddenly, for it may grieve him.

SALERIO

A kinder gentleman treads not the earth;   35
I saw Bassanio and Antonio part;
Bassanio told him he would make some speed
Of his return. He answered, "Do not so;
Slubber not business for my sake, Bassanio,
But stay the very riping of the time,   40
And for the Jew's bond which he hath of me,
Let it not enter in your mind of love.
Be merry, and employ your chiefest thoughts
To courtship, and such fair ostents of love
As shall conveniently become you there."   45
And even there, his eye being big with tears,
Turning his face, he put his hand behind him,

48 *affection wondrous sensible* obvious emotion.

49 *wrung* shook long and hard. This suggests a close friendship.

52 *quicken his embracèd heaviness* try to cheer him up.

Servitor servant.

1 *straight* immediately.

3 *comes...presently* will shortly make his choice.

6 *shall our nuptial rites be solemnized* we shall be married.

8 *hence* here.

9 *enjoined* bound.

And with affection wondrous sensible
He wrung Bassanio's hand, and so they parted.

SOLANIO

I think he only loves the world for him.   50
I pray thee let us go and find him out
And quicken his embracèd heaviness
With some delight or other.

SALERIO

Do we so.

Exeunt

Scene nine

Belmont. A room in Portia's house.

Enter NERISSA *and a Servitor.*

NERISSA

Quick, quick, I pray thee, draw the curtain straight;
The Prince of Arragon hath ta'en his oath,
And comes to his election presently.

A flourish of cornets. Enter the Prince of ARRAGON, *his train, and*
PORTIA.

PORTIA

Behold, there stand the caskets, noble prince;
If you choose that wherein I am contained   5
Straight shall our nuptial rites be solemnized.
But if you fail, without more speech, my lord,
You must be gone from hence immediately.

ARRAGON

I am enjoined by oath to observe three things:–

10 *unfold to anyone* tell anyone.

11–12 *if I fail Of* fail to choose.

17 *injunctions* restrictions, commands.

18 *hazard* guess.

22 *You shall look...hazard* you will have to look better before I am prepared to take a chance on you.

25–6 *that "many"...show* 'many' (the many men of the verse) could mean the foolish majority of people who judge things by their outward appearance.

27 *fond* foolish.

28 *pries not to th'interior* does not see through to the heart of the matter.

martlet housemartin; a bird that nests on the outside of houses, under the eaves.

30 *Even in...casualty* right where it is most dangerous.

32 *jump* go with.

33 *rank...multitudes* class myself with the ignorant hordes of common people.

First, never to unfold to anyone   10
Which casket 't was I chose; next, if I fail
Of the right casket, never in my life
To woo a maid in way of marriage;
Lastly,
If I do fail in fortune of my choice,   15
Immediately to leave you, and be gone.

PORTIA
To these injunctions every one doth swear
That comes to hazard for my worthless self.

ARRAGON
And so have I addressed me – fortune now
To my heart's hope! – Gold, silver, and base lead. 20
"Who chooseth me must give and hazard all he
    hath." –
You shall look fairer, ere I give or hazard.
What says the golden chest? ha! let me see,
"Who chooseth me shall gain what many men
    desire." –
What many men desire – that "many" may be
    meant   25
By the fool multitude that choose by show,
Not learning more than the fond eye doth teach,
Which pries not to th' interior, but, like the martlet,
Builds in the weather on the outward wall,
Even in the force and road of casualty.   30
I will not choose what many men desire,
Because I will not jump with common spirits,
And rank me with the barbarous multitudes.
Why, then, to thee, thou silver treasure house,
Tell me once more what title thou dost bear: 35
"Who chooseth me shall get as much as he
    deserves."

38 *cozen* fool.

39 *stamp of merit* sign that the claim to honour is genuine (like an official stamp).

41 *estates, degrees and offices* belongings, positions of power and respect, and important jobs.

42 *derived corruptly* obtained by devious means.

42–3 *clear honour...wearer* true honour could only be obtained by those that deserved it.

44 *How many...bare!* how many people who now have to take their hats off (in the presence of their masters) would be able to keep their hats on (because they themselves had become masters).

46–7 *How much...honour* how many peasants (people without honour) would be discovered amongst the nobility.

48 *ruin* those who have been ruined.

49 *new-varnished* cleaned up.

51 *assume desert* take what is coming to me.

55 *schedule* a piece of paper.

And well said, too; for who shall go about
To cozen Fortune, and be honourable
Without the stamp of merit? Let none presume
To wear an undeservèd dignity;   40
O that estates, degrees, and offices,
Were not derived corruptly, and that clear
    honour
Were purchased by the merit of the wearer!
How many then should cover that stand bare!
How many be commanded that command!   45
How much low peasantry would then be gleaned
From the true seed of honour! and how much
    honour
Picked from the chaff and ruin of the times,
To be new-varnished! – Well, but to my choice.
"Who chooseth me shall get as much as he
    deserves" –   50
I will assume desert; given me a key for this,
And instantly unlock my fortunes here.

He opens the silver casket.

PORTIA

Too long a pause for that which you find there.

ARRAGON

What's here? the portrait of a blinking idiot
Presenting me a schedule! I will read it.   55
How much unlike art thou to Portia!
How much unlike my hopes and my deservings!
"Who chooseth me shall have as much as he
    deserves"!
Did I deserve no more than a fool's head?
Is that my prize? are my deserts no better?   60

61 *distinct offices*   are separate tasks.

62 *opposèd*   opposing, opposite.

63 *tried this*   tested this (the silver).

65 *amiss*   wrong.

68 *I wis*   without a doubt.

69 *Silvered o'er*   with an attractive outward appearance. It could also mean white-haired and, therefore, people supposed to possess wisdom.

71 *I will ever...head*   the 'blinking idiot' (line 54) will always guide him, or he will always be a fool.

74 *By the time*   all the time.

78 *wroth*   sadness.

80 *deliberate fools!*   people who deliberate or think hard before going on to act foolishly.

81 *They have...to lose*   they have just got enough sense to use their powers of reasoning to let them lose.

82 *heresy*   opinion opposite to that normally held.

PORTIA

To offend and judge are distinct offices,
And of opposèd natures.

ARRAGON

What is here?
(*He reads from the scroll*) *The fire seven times
tried this;
Seven times tried that judgement is
That did never choose amiss* 65
*Some there be that shadows kiss;
Such have but a shadow's bliss.
There be fools alive, I wis,
Silvered o'er, and so was this.
Take what wife you will to bed,* 70
*I will ever be your head.
So be gone; you are sped.*

Still more fool I shall appear
By the time I linger here;
With one fool's head I came to woo, 75
But I go away with two.
Sweet, adieu! I'll keep my oath,
Patiently to bear my wroth.

Exit ARRAGON *with his train*

PORTIA

Thus hath the candle singed the moth;
O these deliberate fools! when they do choose, 80
They have the wisdom by their wit to lose.

NERISSA

The ancient saying is no heresy,
Hanging and wiving goes by destiny.

85 *what would* what do you want?

my lord Portia is responding to the servant's use of 'my lady'.

89 *sensible regreets* ample (both in terms of words and gifts) greetings.

90 *To wit* that is.

commends and courteous breath praise and polite phrases.

92 *ambassador* messenger.

95 *fore-spurrer* horseman who spurs his horse ahead of the rest of the people he travels with.

96 *afeard* afraid.

97 *anon* soon.

some kin to thee related to you.

98 *high-day wit* elaborate speech.

100 *Cupid* the son of Venus, the goddess of love, who was said to fire arrows at humans and thus make them fall in love.

post messenger.

so mannerly so stylishly.

101 *Bassanio...be* Cupid, if it is what you want, please let it be Bassanio.

PORTIA

Come, draw the curtain, Nerissa.

Enter MESSENGER.

MESSENGER

Where is my lady?

PORTIA

       Here; what would my lord? 85

MESSENGER

Madam, there is alighted at your gate
A young Venetian, one that comes before
To signify th' approaching of his lord,
From whom he bringeth sensible regreets,
To wit, besides commends and courteous breath, 90
Gifts of rich value. Yet I have not seen
So likely an ambassador of love.
A day in April never came so sweet
To show how costly summer was at hand,
As this fore-spurrer comes before his lord. 95

PORTIA

No more, I pray thee; I am half afeard
Thou wilt say anon he is some kin to thee,
Thou spend'st such high-day wit in praising him.
Come, come Nerissa for I long to see
Quick Cupid's post that comes so mannerly. 100

NERISSA

Bassanio, Lord Love, if thy will it be!

            Exeunt

Bassanio and Portia: Royal Shakespeare Company, 1981 (Christopher Pearce/The Panic Pictures Library).

Act 3: summary

Bassanio correctly chooses the lead casket and wins Portia's hand in marriage. Portia gives him a ring and makes him promise to wear it always. Everything appears to be wonderful as Gratiano has also managed to persuade Nerissa to marry him. However, this happy mood is shattered when a messenger arrives with a letter from Antonio.

The letter tells Bassanio that all Antonio's ships have been lost at sea, he cannot repay Shylock and he would dearly like to see Bassanio before he dies at the hands of the moneylender. Portia insists that Bassanio leaves for Venice at once with enough gold to pay back Shylock's loan. Once her husband has left, however, she makes her own plans. Lorenzo and Jessica are left in charge of her household, whilst she sends a message to her cousin, the lawyer Doctor Bellario.

She then tells Nerissa that they too will go to Venice, disguised as men.

1 *the Rialto*   meeting place where Venetian gentlemen and merchants did business.

2 *It lives there unchecked*   the story is not being denied.

3 *lading*   cargo.

4 *the Goodwins*   the Goodwin sands in the English Channel.

5 *flat*   sand-bank.

6–7 *my gossip...word*   a gossip was an unflattering name for an old woman. Here, Salerio uses it to conjure up a picture of the rumours that are being spread around the market place, almost as if such a woman were running around telling everyone.

9 *knapped ginger*   nibbled ginger (a habit associated with old women in Shakespeare's time).

11 *slips of prolixity*   making the mistake of being longwinded.

11–12 *crossing the plain highway of talk*   leaving the road of simple, clear speech.

15 *Come, the full stop*   get to the point, finish what you have to say.

Act Three

Scene one

Venice. A street.

Enter SOLANIO *and* SALERIO.

SOLANIO
Now what news on the Rialto?

SALERIO
Why, yet it lives there unchecked, that Antonio
hath a ship of rich lading wrecked on the narrow
seas – the Goodwins, I think they call the place, a
very dangerous flat, and fatal, where the carcases of   5
many a tall ship lie buried, as they say – if my gossip
Report be an honest woman of her word.

SOLANIO
I would she were as lying a gossip in that as ever
knapped ginger, or made her neighbours believe she
wept for the death of a third husband. But it is true,   10
without any slips of prolixity, or crossing the plain
highway of talk, that the good Antonio, the honest
Antonio – O that I had a title good enough to keep
his name company! –

SALERIO
Come, the full stop.   15

SOLANIO
Ha! what sayest thou? – why the end is, he hath lost
a ship.

19 *amen*   so be it. A word said at the end of prayers.

betimes   immediately.

lest   unless, in case.

19–20 *cross my prayer*   spoil my prayer (the prayer being 'amen').

26 *wings*   the disguise that Jessica wore when she became Lorenzo's torch-bearer. Salerio picks up Shylock's use of the word 'flight' for escape, and Solanio (in the next speech) continues the image of a young bird flying the nest.

28 *fledged*   could fly.

28–9 *it is the complexion...dam*   it is only natural that they leave their mother (parents) when they are grown up.

31 *the devil...judge*   the use of the word 'devil' here could either mean Satan or Shylock himself.

33 *carrion*   rotting flesh.

rebels...years   Solanio is talking about Shylock's flesh and blood here, rather than Jessica which is what Shylock meant. Solanio suggests that Shylock is losing control over himself because of his age.

SALERIO

I would it might prove the end of his losses.

SOLANIO

Let me say "amen" betimes, lest the devil cross my
prayer, for here he comes in the likeness of a Jew. 20

Enter SHYLOCK.

How now, Shylock! what news among the merchants?

SHYLOCK

You knew, none so well, none so well as you, of my
daughter's flight.

SALERIO

That's certain; I, for my part, knew the tailor that 25
made the wings she flew withal.

SOLANIO

Any Shylock, for his own part, knew the bird was
fledged, and then it is the complexion of them all to
leave the dam.

SHYLOCK

She is damned for it.   30

SALERIO

That's certain, if the devil may be her judge.

SHYLOCK

My own flesh and blood to rebel!

SOLANIO

Out upon it, old carrion! rebels it at these years?

SHYLOCK

I say my daughter is my flesh and my blood.

36 *jet and ivory*   jet is a black stone and ivory the white horn of elephants' tusks, both used to make jewellery. Salerio is saying that Shylock and Jessica are as different as black and white.

37 *Rhenish*   white wine from Germany.

40 *bad match*   bad bargain. The other 'bad match' was that of Jessica and Lorenzo
    prodigal   someone who spends their money too freely.

42–3 *that was used...mart*   who used to be so self-satisfied when he came to do business.

43 *was wont to*   used to, liked to.

47 *forfeit*   cannot pay you.

49 *To bait fish withal*   Shylock will use Antonio's flesh as fish bait if he chooses to do so.

51 *hindered...million*   Shylock estimates that Antonio has stopped him making half a million ducats.

52 *scorned my nation*   made mockery of the fact that I am a Jew.
    thwarted   spoilt.

53–4 *cooled...enemies*   turned by friends against me, and encouraged my enemies.

55–6 *dimensions*   a physical form that can be measured.

56 *affections*   desires.
    passions   strong emotions; a logical consequence of desiring.

SALERIO

There is more difference between thy flesh and hers 35
than between jet and ivory, more between your
bloods than there is between red wine and Rhenish.
But tell us, do you hear whether Antonio have had
any loss at sea or no?

SHYLOCK

There I have another bad match, a bankrupt, a prodi- 40
gal, who dare scarce show his head on the Rialto,
a beggar that was used to come so smug upon the
mart. Let him look to his bond! He was wont to call
me usurer; let him look to his bond! He was wont to
lend money for a Christian courtesy; let him look to 45
his bond!

SALERIO

Why, I am sure, if he forfeit, thou wilt not take his
flesh – what's *that* good for?

SHYLOCK

To bait fish withal; – if it will feed nothing else, it
will feed my revenge. He hath disgraced me, and 50
hindered me half a million – laughed at my losses,
mocked at my gains, scorned my nation, thwarted
my bargains, cooled my friends, heated mine enemies – and what's his reason? I am a Jew. Hath not
a Jew eyes? hath not a Jew hands, organs, dimen- 55
sions, senses, affections, passions? fed with the same
food, hurt with the same weapons, subject to the
same diseases, healed by the same means, warmed
and cooled by the same winter and summer as a
Christian is? If you prick us, do we not bleed? If you 60
tickle us, do we not laugh? if you poison us, do we
not die? – And if you wrong us, shall we not revenge?

65 *humility*   patience, correct Christian action in the face of hostility.

66 *sufferance*   patient suffering.

67–9 *The villainy...instruction*   I shall follow your teaching (by taking revenge) and although it might not be easy I will do better than my teachers.

75 *Genoa*   an important sea port in Italy.

80 *Frankfort*   a city and centre of trade in Germany.

80–2 *the curse...till now*   the Jews were generally believed to be cursed as a race because of the part they played in the crucifixion of Christ.

If we are like you in the rest, we will resemble you in that. If a Jew wrong a Christian, what is his humility? Revenge! If a Christian wrong a Jew, what 65 should his sufferance be by Christian example? Why, revenge! The villainy you teach me I will execute, and it shall go hard but I will better the instruction.

Enter a SERVING-MAN *from* ANTONIO.

SERVING-MAN

Gentlemen, my master Antonio is at his house, and 70 desires to speak with you both.

SALERIO

We have been up and down to seek him.

Enter TUBAL.

SOLANIO

Here comes another of the tribe; a third cannot be matched unless the devil himself turn Jew.

Exeunt SOLANIO *and* SALERIO *with the* SERVING-MAN

SHYLOCK

How now, Tubal! what news from Genoa? has thou 75 found my daughter?

TUBAL

I often came where I did hear of her, but cannot find her.

SHYLOCK

Why there, there, there, there! A diamond gone cost me two thousand ducats in Frankfort – the curse 80 never fell upon our nation till now, I never felt it till now – two thousand ducats in that and other pre-

85 *hearsed*   in a coffin.
90 *lights*   comes to rest on.
96 *cast away*   shipwrecked.
103 *fourscore*   eighty.

cious, precious jewels. I would my daughter were
dead at my foot, and the jewels in her ear; would she
were hearsed at my foot, and the ducats in her 85
coffin. – No news of them? why, so! – and I know
not what's spent in the search: why thou – loss upon
loss! The thief gone with so much, and so much to
find the thief, and no satisfaction, no revenge, nor
no ill luck stirring but what lights on *my* shoulders, 90
no sighs but of *my* breathing, no tears but of *my*
shedding.

TUBAL

Yes, other men have ill luck too – Antonio, as I
heard in Genoa, –

SHYLOCK

What, what, what? ill luck, ill luck? 95

TUBAL

– hath an argosy cast away coming from Tripolis.

SHYLOCK

I thank God, I thank God! Is it true, is it true?

TUBAL

I spoke with some of the sailors that escaped the
wreck.

SHYLOCK

I thank thee, good Tubal; good news, good news: ha 100
ha! heard in Genoa!

TUBAL

Your daughter spent in Genoa, as I heard, one
night, fourscore ducats.

SHYLOCK

Thou stick'st a dagger in me – I shall never see my

105 *a sitting*   at one time.

107 *divers*   a variety.

109 *but break*   become bankrupt.

114 *Out upon her*   curse her!

115 *Leah*   Shylock's dead wife. This is the only time that she is mentioned.

118 *undone*   ruined.

119–20 *fee me an officer*   pay for an officer.

120 *bespeak him...before*   book his services two weeks before (Antonio is due to pay the money back). The officer will then be on hand to arrest Antonio when he fails to pay his debts.

121 *forfeit*   fails to pay.

121–2 *for were...I will*   if Antonio were not in Venice then I would be able to run my business deals without interference.

123 *synagogue*   a place of worship for Jews.

gold again – fourscore ducats at a sitting, fourscore 105
ducats!

TUBAL

There came divers of Antonio's creditors in my
company to Venice, that swear he cannot choose
but break.

SHYLOCK

I am very glad of it – I'll plague him, I'll torture 110
him – I am glad of it.

TUBAL

One of them showed me a ring that he had of your
daughter for a monkey.

SHYLOCK

Out upon her! – Thou torturest me, Tubal – it was
my turquoise; I had it of Leah when I was a bach- 115
elor. I would not have given it for a wilderness of
monkeys.

TUBAL

But Antonio is certainly undone.

SHYLOCK

Nay, that's true, that's very true. – Go, Tubal, fee
me an officer, bespeak him a fortnight before – I will 120
have the heart of him if he forfeit, for were he out of
Venice I can make what merchandise I will. Go,
Tubal, and meet me at our synagogue – go, good
Tubal – at our synagogue, Tubal.

Exeunt

1 *tarry* wait.

2 *hazard* hazard a guess, choose.

3 *forbear* wait, hesitate.

6 *Hate...quality* hatred does not give this kind of advice.

7 *lest* unless, in case.

8 *hath no tongue but thought* is better at keeping her thoughts to herself, rather than speaking out.

10 *venture* attempt the task (of solving the riddle).

11 *I am forsworn* I would have broken the oath I swore.

14 *Beshrew* damn.

18 *naughty* wicked.

19 *bars* obstacles.

20 *though yours, not yours* Portia's heart belongs to Bassanio already because she is in love with him. However, until he solves the riddle of the caskets she is not free to marry him.

Prove it so if it happens like that.

22 *peize* piece out, divide up and therefore increase.

23 *eche it* eke it out, to stretch it so that it lasts longer.

24 *To stay you from election* to keep you from having to make the choice.

Scene two

Belmont. A room in Portia's house.

Enter BASSANIO, PORTIA, GRATIANO, NERISSA, *and all their trains.*

PORTIA

 I pray you, tarry; pause a day or two
 Before you hazard, for in choosing wrong
 I lose your company; therefore forbear a while.
 There's something tells me – but it is not love –
 I would not lose you; and you know yourself,   5
 Hate counsels not in such a quality.
 But lest you should not understand me well –
 And yet a maiden hath no tongue but thought –
 I would detain you here some month or two
 Before you venture for me. I could teach you   10
 How to choose right, but then I am forsworn;
 So will I never be; so may you miss me;
 But if you do, you'll make me wish a sin,
 That I had been forsworn. Beshrew your eyes;
 They have o'erlooked me and divided me;   15
 One half of me is yours, the other half yours –
 Mine own I would say; but if mine, then yours,
 And so all yours. O, these naughty times
 Put bars between the owners and their rights!
 And so though yours, not yours. Prove it so,   20
 Let Fortune go to hell for it, not I.
 I speak too long, but 't is to peize the time,
 To eche it, and to draw it out in length,
 To stay you from election.

25 *I live upon the rack*   the suspense is like being tortured.

27 *treason*   this is linked with the idea of torturing a confession out of someone by using the rack, but Portia also wants to know why Bassanio is not completely happy in her company.

29 *fear th'enjoying*   he is afraid of enjoying his love because his situation is not yet secure and he may yet lose Portia.

30 *amity*   friendship.

33 *enforcèd*   forced, tortured.

38 *answers for deliverance*   the answers that will stop the torture.

42 *aloof*   apart, aside.

44 *a swan-like end*   according to legend, swans were supposed to sing beautifully just before their death (hence the term 'swan-song').

BASSANIO

                          Let me choose,
For as I am, I live upon the rack.   25

PORTIA

Upon the rack, Bassanio? then confess
What treason there is mingled with your love.

BASSANIO

None but that ugly treason of mistrust,
Which makes me fear th' enjoying of my love.
There may as well be amity and life   30
'Tween snow and fire, as treason and my love.

PORTIA

Ay, but I fear you speak upon the rack
Where men enforcèd do speak anything.

BASSANIO

Promise me life, and I'll confess the truth.

PORTIA

Well then, confess and live.

BASSANIO

                      "Confess and love"   35
Had been the very sum of my confession.
O happy torment, when my torturer
Doth teach me answers for deliverance!
But let me to my fortune and the caskets.

PORTIA

Away then! I am locked in one of them;   40
If you do love me, you will find me out.
Nerissa and the rest, stand all aloof!
Let music sound while he doth make his choice;
Then if he lose he makes a swan-like end,

45–6 *That the comparison...proper*   so that this image (of the dying swan) is even more suitable.

46–7 *my eye...for him*   my tears will provide the water (that the swan would have been swimming on).

49 *the flourish*   fanfare, a short burst of music.

50 *monarch*   king or queen.

51 *dulcet*   sweet.

55 *Alcides*   Hercules. In one of his many adventures this Greek hero saved a princess of Troy called Hesoine, who had been chained to a rock as an offering for a sea monster.

57–60 *I stand...exploit*   Portia compares herself to the princess, whilst the other people present represent the women of Troy ('the Dardanian wives') who stand, their faces wet with tears ('blearèd visages') awaiting the outcome of the contest.

62 *fray*   battle.

63 *Fancy*   an attraction to something that is not based on logical reasoning, often seen as being foolish.

65 *begot*   born.

    nourishèd   fed, looked after.

67 *engendered*   begins, is conceived.

70 *knell*   a death bell.

Fading in music. That the comparison 45
May stand more proper, my eye shall be the stream
And wat'ry death-bed for him. He may win,
And what is music then? Then music is
Even as the flourish, when true subjects bow
To a new-crownèd monarch; such it is, 50
As are those dulcet sounds in break of day
That creep into the dreaming bridegroom's ear,
And summon him to marriage. Now he goes,
With no less presence, but with much more love,
Than young Alcides, when he did redeem 55
The virgin tribute, paid by howling Troy
To the sea-monster. I stand for sacrifice;
The rest aloof are the Dardanian wives,
With blearèd visages come forth to view
The issue of th' exploit. Go, Hercules! 60
Live thou, I live; with much, much more dismay,
I view the fight, than thou that mak'st the fray.

A song to music whilst BASSANIO *comments on the caskets to himself.*

> *Tell me where is Fancy bred,*
> *Or in the heart, or in the head?*
> *How begot, how nourishèd?* 65

ALL

Reply, reply.

> *It is engendered in the eyes,*
> *With gazing fed, and Fancy dies*
> *In the cradle where it lies.*
> *Let us all ring Fancy's knell;* 70
> *I'll begin it, – Ding, dong, bell.*

ALL

Ding, dong, bell.

73 *be least themselves* are not truthful.

74 *with ornament* with the appearance of things.

76 *being seasoned...evil* by being presented with a pleasant voice the evil is hidden.

78 *sober brow* serious person, scholar.

79 *approve it with a text* quote from the Bible to show there is support for the mistake.

82 *Some mark...parts* some appearance of good.

83–6 *How many...as milk* how many cowards are there who have no inner strength? They may look as brave as the ancient heroes but when you investigate further you find that they are completely lacking in courage.

87 *valour's excrement* the least valuable part of bravery, i.e. outward show.

88 *render* make them appear.

redoubted unbeatable.

89–90 *purchased...nature* a reference to make-up, which again is only an outward show of beauty.

92 *crispèd* curled.

93 *wanton* carefree.

gambols movements.

95–6 *the dowry of...sepulchre* a wig made from hair cut from someone who is now dead and in the 'sepulchre'.

98 *guilèd shore* a stretch of shore that may appear beautiful but is, in reality, dangerous.

99 *Indian beauty* i.e. someone who is not beautiful at all. The Elizabethans believed pale skin was a sign of beauty.

100 *put on* assumes.

102 *Midas* a king in Greek legend who was granted the ability to turn everything he touched into gold. Not surprisingly this caused considerable problems when he tried to eat!

103 *drudge* servant (because money is made from silver).

104 *meagre* poor.

105 *aught* anything.

BASSANIO

So may the outward shows be least themselves;
The world is still deceived with ornament.
In law, what plea so tainted and corrupt,   75
But, being seasoned with a gracious voice,
Obscures the show of evil? In religion,
What damnèd error but some sober brow
Will bless it, and approve it with a text,
Hiding the grossness with fair ornament?   80
There is no vice so simple, but assumes
Some mark of virtue on his outward parts.
How many cowards whose hearts are all as false
As stairs of sand, wear yet upon their chins
The beards of Hercules and frowning Mars,   85
Who, inward searched, have livers white as milk?
And these assume but valour's excrement
To render them redoubted. Look on beauty,
And you shall see 't is purchased by the weight,
Which therein works a miracle in nature,   90
Making them lightest that wear most of it;
So are those crispèd, snaky golden locks
Which make such wanton gambols with the wind
Upon supposèd fairness, often known
To be the dowry of a second head,   95
The skull that bred them in the sepulchre.
Thus ornament is but the guilèd shore
To a most dangerous sea, the beauteous scarf
Veiling an Indian beauty – in a word,
The seeming truth which cunning times put on   100
To entrap the wisest. Therefore, thou gaudy gold,
Hard food for Midas, I will none of thee,
Nor none of thee, thou pale and common drudge
'Tween man and man. But thou, thou meagre lead,
Which rather threaten'st than dost promise aught, 105

106 *eloquence*   skill with words.

108 *fleet to air*   vanish into thin air.

111 *allay thy ecstasy*   calm yourself.

112 *In measure...excess*   let me experience this joy in a sensible, moderate quantity; hold back this excessive outpouring of emotion.

114 *surfeit*   overindulge.

115 *counterfeit*   copy.

demi-god   a minor god, or a human with god-like qualities.

117 *balls*   eyeballs.

118 *severed*   parted, open.

119 *so sweet a bar*   her breath.

120 *sunder*   drive apart.

sweet friends   her lips.

122 *mesh*   net.

124 *having made one...unfurnished*   having painted one of Portia's eyes Bassanio says that the painted eye should have had the power to steal the gift of sight from both of the eyes belonging to the painter, thus making it impossible to finish the portrait.

127–9 *The substance...the substance*   my praise is unworthy of the true beauty of the portrait; just as the portrait is unworthy of Portia's beauty.

130 *continent*   summary.

Thy paleness moves me more than eloquence,
And here choose I; joy be the consequence!

PORTIA *(Aside)*

How all the other passions fleet to air,
As doubtful thoughts, and rash-embraced despair,
And shudd'ring fear, and green-eyed jealousy.   110
O love, be moderate, allay thy ecstasy!
In measure rain thy join, scant this excess!
I feel too much thy blessing; make it less
For fear I surfeit!

BASSANIO

What find I here?

He opens the lead casket.

Fair Portia's counterfeit! What demi-god   115
Hath come so near creation? Move these eyes?
Or whether (riding on the balls of mine)
Seem they in motion? Here are severed lips
Parted with sugar breath; so sweet a bar
Should sunder such sweet friends. Here in her hairs 120
The painter plays the spider, and hath woven
A golden mesh t' entrap the hearts of men
Faster than gnats in cobwebs. But her eyes!
How could he see to do them? having made one,
Methinks it should have power to steal both his   125
And leave itself unfurnished. Yet look how far
The substance of my praise doth wrong this shadow
In underprizing it, so far this shadow
Doth limp behind the substance. Here's the scroll,
The continent and summary of my fortune.   130

> *You that choose not by the view,*
> *Chance as fair, and choose as true!*

137

140 *by note* by the words on the scroll.

141 *contending in a prize* competing in a contest.

145 *peals* shouts.

146 *thrice-fair* beautiful three times over.

148 *ratified* officially approved.

150–2 *for myself...much better* I am not so ambitious as to wish myself better tha
am merely for my own desires.

153 *trebled twenty times myself* I would like my value to be increased by twent
times and then have that trebled again.

155 *high in your account* high in your estimation, opinion. Note the use of
language to do with business and money here.

157–8 *But the full sum...something* Portia hesitates to sum up her own worth.

158 *in gross* in total. It could also mean to speak plainly.

Since this fortune falls to you,
Be content, and seek no new.
If you be well pleased with this, 135
And hold your fortune for your bliss,
Turn you where your lady is,
And claim her with a loving kiss.

A gentle scroll. Fair lady, by your leave,
I come by note to give, and to receive. 140
(*He kisses her*) Like one of two contending in a prize
That thinks he hath done well in people's eyes,
Hearing applause and universal shout,
Giddy in spirit, still gazing in a doubt
Whether those peals of praise be his or no, 145
So, thrice-fair lady, stand I even so,
As doubtful whether what I see be true,
Until confirmed, signed, ratified by you.

PORTIA
You see me, Lord Bassanio, where I stand,
Such as I am; though for myself alone 150
I would not be ambitious in my wish
To wish myself much better, yet for you,
I would be trebled twenty times myself,
A thousand times more fair, ten thousand times
    more rich,
That only to stand high in your account, 155
I might in virtues, beauties, livings, friends
Exceed account. But the full sum of me
Is sum of – something: which, to term in gross,
Is an unlessoned girl, unschooled, unpractised;
Happy in this, she is not yet so old 160
But she may learn; happier than this,
She is not bred so dull but she can learn;
Happiest of all, is that her gentle spirit

167   *converted*   changed. Portia has just given Bassanio authority over all she owns.

169   *even now, but now*   in this moment.

173   *presage*   herald.

174   *vantage*   chance.

175   *bereft me*   taken from me.

177   *powers*   ability to think.

178   *oration*   formal speech.

181–3   *Where every...expressed*   all individual expressions of happiness coming together make one loud noise that only conveys the general atmosphere of joy, rather than the individual emotion.

Commits itself to yours to be directed,
As from her lord, her governor, her king.   165
Myself, and what is mine, to you and yours
Is now converted. But now I was the lord
Of this fair mansion, master of my servants,
Queen o'er myself; and even now, but now,
This house, these servants, and this same myself   170
Are yours, my lord! I give them with this ring,
Which when you part from, lose, or give away,
Let it presage the ruin of your love,
And be my vantage to exclaim on you.

BASSANIO

Madam, you have bereft me of all words;   175
Only my blood speaks to you in my veins,
And there is such confusion in my powers,
As after some oration fairly spoke
By a belovèd prince, there doth appear
Among the buzzing pleasèd multitude –   180
Where every something being blent together,
Turns to a wild of nothing, save of joy
Expressed, and not expressed. But when this ring
Parts from this finger, then parts life from hence; –
O, then be bold to say Bassanio's dead!   185

NERISSA

My lord and lady, it is now our time
That have stood by and seen our wishes prosper,
To cry "good joy". Good joy, my lord and lady!

GRATIANO

My lord Bassanio, and my gentle lady,
I wish you all the joy that *you* can wish;   190
For I am sure you can wish none from me.

192–3 *solemnize...faith*   get married.

195 *so thou canst*   if you can.

197 *swift*   fast.

199–200 *for intermission...than you*   'intermission' means to wait. Gratiano is
saying that Bassanio was not slow in getting himself a wife and neither was he

202 *as the matter falls*   as things have happened.

203–5 *until I sweat...of love*   by means of a lot of hard work (which made me sweat)
and making so many promises of love that my mouth became dry.

207–8 *your fortune Achieved*   you were lucky enough to win.

209 *so you stand pleased withal*   if this is all right with you.

And when your honours mean to solemnize
The bargain of your faith, I do beseech you
Even at that time I may be married too.

BASSANIO

With all my heart, so thou canst get a wife.   195

GRATIANO

I thank your lordship, you have got me one.
My eyes, my lord, can look as swift as yours:
You saw the mistress, I beheld the maid;
You loved, I loved; – for intermission
No more pertains to me, my lord, than you.   200
Your fortune stood upon the caskets there,
And so did mine too, as the matter falls;
For wooing here until I sweat again,
And swearing till my very roof was dry
With oaths of love, at last, if promise last,   205
I got a promise of this fair one here
To have her love, provided that your fortune
Achieved her mistress.

PORTIA

                    Is this true, Nerissa?

NERISSA

Madam, it is, so you stand pleased withal.

BASSANIO

And do you, Gratiano, mean good faith?   210

GRATIANO

Yes, faith, my lord.

BASSANIO

Our feast shall be much honoured in your marriage.

213–4 *We'll play...ducats*   we'll have a bet with them. The first couple to have a baby boy gets a thousand ducats from the other couple.

215 *stake*   the thousand ducats that must be found for the bet.

217 *his infidel*   Jessica.

220–1 *the youth...welcome*   Bassanio automatically greets his friends and then remembers that he has only just acquired authority over Portia and her household.

228 *entreat*   beg.

past all saying nay   so that it was impossible to refuse.

231 *Commends him to you*   greets you.

GRATIANO

We'll play with them the first boy for a thousand
ducats.

NERISSA

What! and stake down?   215

GRATIANO

No, we shall ne'er win at that sport and stake down.
But who comes here? Lorenzo and his infidel!
What! and my old Venetian friend Salerio?

Enter LORENZO, JESSICA, *and* SALERIO.

BASSANIO

Lorenzo and Salerio, welcome hither,
If that the youth of my new int'rest here   220
Have power to bid you welcome. By your leave
I bid my very friends and countrymen,
Sweet Portia, welcome.

PORTIA

              So do I my lord;
They are entirely welcome.

LORENZO

I thank your honour. – For my part, my lord,   225
My purpose was not to have seen you here,
But meeting with Salerio by the way,
He did entreat me, past all saying nay,
To come with him along.

SALERIO

              I did, my lord,
And I have reason for it. Signior Antonio   230
Commends him to you.

He gives BASSANIO *a letter.*

231 *Ere I ope*   before I open.

233 *Not sick...mind*   outwardly Antonio appears unchanged. Any changes, whether in sickness or health, must have taken place mentally.

235 *his estate*   his situation, state.

236 *yon*   that.

240 *Jasons*   see note to Act 1, scene 1, line 170.

242 *shrewd*   evil.

245–6 *Could turn...man*   could alter the appearance (by making him lose his colour) of a healthy man.

247 *With leave*   with your permission.

252 *impart my love to you*   tell you of my love for you.

BASSANIO

                    Ere I ope his letter,
I pray you tell me how my good friend doth.

SALERIO

Not sick, my lord, unless it be in mind,
Nor well, unless in mind; his letter there
Will show you his estate.   235

BASSANIO *opens the letter.*

GRATIANO

Nerissa, cheer yon stranger, bid her welcome.
Your hand, Salerio (*They shake hands*) what's the news
    from Venice?
How doth that royal merchant, good Antonio?
I know he will be glad of our success;
We are the Jasons, we have won the fleece.   240

SALERIO

I would you had won the fleece that he hath lost.

PORTIA

There are some shrewd contents in yon same paper,
That steals the colour from Bassanio's cheek –
Some dear friend dead, else nothing in the world
Could turn so much the constitution   245
Of any constant man. What, worse and worse?
With leave, Bassanio, I am half yourself,
And I must freely have the half of anything
That this same paper brings you.

BASSANIO

                O sweet Portia,
Here are a few of the unpleasant'st words   250
That ever blotted paper! Gentle lady,
When I did first impart my love to you,

253–4 *the wealth...veins*   in other words his blood was good (he came from a good family) but he had no money.

256 *Rating myself*   assessing myself.

257 *a braggart*   a boastful man.

260 *have engaged*   am indebted.

261 *mere*   complete.

262 *feed my means*   provide me with what I need (money).

266 *ventures*   business deals.

one hit   one success.

270 *merchant-marring*   rocks that ruin merchants by ruining their ships.

272 *present money*   money available right now.

discharge   pay off.

275 *confound*   bring down.

276 *plies*   hounds, besieges with requests.

277–8 *impeach...justice*   call into question the justice of the state if he is not allowed to pursue his case.

279–80 *magnificoes ... port*   the most important and dignified men.

280 *persuaded with him*   tried to persuade him.

281 *envious*   malicious, done with evil intent.

282 *forfeiture*   failing to keep an agreement.

I freely told you all the wealth I had
Ran in my veins – I was a gentleman;
And then I told you true. And yet, dear lady,   255
Rating myself at nothing, you shall see
How much I was a braggart. – When I told you
My state was nothing, I should then have told you
That I was worse than nothing; for indeed
I have engaged myself to a dear friend,   260
Engaged my friend to his mere enemy
To feed my means. Here is a letter, lady;
The paper as the body of my friend,
And every word in it a gaping wound
Issuing life-blood. But is it true, Salerio?   265
Hath *all* his ventures failed? what, not *one* hit?
From Tripolis, from Mexico, and England,
From Lisbon, Barbary, and India,
And not one vessel scape the dreadful touch
Of merchant-marring rocks?

SALERIO

               Not one, my lord.   270
Besides, it should appear that if he had
The present money to discharge the Jew,
He would not take it. Never did I know
A creature that did bear the shape of man
So keen and greedy to confound a man.   275
He plies the duke at morning and at night,
And doth impeach the freedom of the state
If they deny him justice. Twenty merchants,
The duke himself, and the magnificoes
Of greatest port have all persuaded with him,   280
But none can drive him from the envious plea
Of forfeiture, of justice, and his bond.

288 *deny not*   do not prevent it.

289 *go hard*   go badly.

292–3 *The best-conditioned...courtesies*   a man of the finest quality who is tireless when it comes to doing things for other people.

294 *The ancient Roman honour*   the virtue of honour or integrity which was highly prized by the Romans.

298 *deface the bond*   pay off, cancel out.

JESSICA

When I was with him I have heard him swear
To Tubal and to Chus, his countrymen,
That he would rather have Antonio's flesh   285
Than twenty times the value of the sum
That he did owe him. And I know, my lord,
If law, authority, and power deny not,
It will go hard with poor Antonio.

PORTIA

Is it your dear friend that is thus in trouble?   290

BASSANIO

The dearest friend to me, the kindest man,
The best-conditioned and unwearied spirit
In doing courtesies, and one in whom
The ancient Roman honour more appears
Than any that draws breath in Italy.   295

PORTIA

What sum owes he the Jew?

BASSANIO

For me, three thousand ducats.

PORTIA

                                    What, no more?
Pay him six thousand, and deface the bond;
Double six thousand, and then treble that,
Before a friend of this description   300
Shall lose a hair through Bassanio's fault.
First go with me to church, and call me wife,
And then away to Venice to your friend;
For never shall you lie by Portia's side
With an unquiet soul. You shall have gold   305
To pay the petty debt twenty times over.

312   *dear bought*   i.e. you have cost me a lot.

314   *miscarried*   been wrecked.

      creditors   people with whom he has debts.

315   *my estate is very low*   I have very little (both money and property) left.

318   *use your pleasure*   do as you wish.

320   *dispatch all business*   make all the arrangements.

321   *good leave*   permission.

322   *stay*   waiting, delay.

324   *Nor rest be interposer...twain*   I will not rest until I see you again.

When it is paid, bring your true friend along. –
My maid Nerissa and myself meantime
Will live as maids and widows. – Come, away!
For you shall hence upon your wedding day.   310
Bid your friends welcome; show a merry cheer –
Since you are dear bought, I will love you dear.
But let me hear the letter of your friend.

BASSANIO (*Reads*)
Sweet Bassanio, my ships have all miscarried, my creditors
grow cruel, my estate is very low, my bond to the Jew is 315
forfeit, and, since in paying it it is impossible I should live,
all debts are cleared between you and I, if I might but see you
at my death. Notwithstanding, use your pleasure; if your
love do not persuade you to come, let not my letter.

PORTIA
O love, dispatch all business and be gone!   320

BASSANIO
Since I have your good leave to go away,
I will make haste; but, till I come again,
No bed shall e'er be guilty of my stay,
Nor rest be interposer 'twixt us twain.

Exeunt

Scene three

Venice. A street.

Enter SHYLOCK *the Jew, with* SOLANIO, *and* ANTONIO, *and a*
GAOLER.

SHYLOCK
Gaoler, look to him; tell not me of mercy;

2 *gratis*   (Latin) without charging interest.

9 *naughty*   wicked.

art so fond   so indulgent.

10 *come abroad*   come out (of the jail).

14 *dull-eyed*   gullible, easily fooled.

16 *intercessors*   people who plead on other people's behalf.

18 *impenetrable cur*   hard (hearted) dog.

19 *kept with men*   lived with men.

20 *bootless*   pointless.

This is the fool that lent out money gratis.
Gaoler, look to him.

ANTONIO

     Hear me yet, good Shylock.

SHYLOCK

I'll have my bond; speak not against my bond –
I have sworn an oath that I will have my bond. 5
Thou call'dst me dog before thou hadst a cause,
But since I am a dog, beware my fangs –
The duke shall grant me justice – I do wonder,
Thou naughty gaoler, that thou art so fond
To come abroad with him at his request. 10

ANTONIO

I pray thee hear me speak.

SHYLOCK

I'll have my bond. I will not hear thee speak;
I'll have my bond, and therefore speak no more.
I'll not be made a soft and dull-eyed fool,
To shake the head, relent, and sigh, and yield 15
To Christian intercessors. (*He turns to go*) Follow
  not –
I'll have no speaking; I will have my bond.

              Exit

SOLANIO

It is the most impenetrable cur
That ever kept with men.

ANTONIO

     Let him alone;
I'll follow him no more with bootless prayers. 20
He seeks my life, his reason well I know;

22–3 *I oft delivered...to me* I have often helped those who owed him money when they came to me and asked for aid.

26–31 *The duke...all nations* the Duke will have to uphold the law because if he does not do so then Venice's reputation for justice will mean nothing to the many people who come to trade here.

32 *bated* made sad (and therefore thinner).

2 *conceit* concept of.

3 *amity* friendship.

I oft delivered from his forfeitures
Many that have at times made moan to me;
Therefore he hates me.

SOLANIO

                I am sure the duke
Will never grant this forfeiture to hold.   25

ANTONIO

The duke cannot deny the course of law;
For the commodity that strangers have
With us in Venice, if it be denied,
Will much impeach the justice of the state,
Since that the trade and profit of the city   30
Consisteth of all nations. Therefore go. –
These griefs and losses have so bated me
That I shall hardly spare a pound of flesh
To-morrow, to my bloody creditor.
Well gaoler, on. – Pray God Bassanio come   35
To see me pay his debt, and then I care not.

Exeunt

Scene four

Belmont. A room in Portia's house.

Enter PORTIA, NERISSA, LORENZO, JESSICA, *and* BALTHAZAR.

LORENZO

Madam, although I speak it in your presence,
You have a noble and a true conceit
Of god-like amity, which appears most strongly
In bearing thus the absence of your lord.
But if you knew to whom you show this honour,   5

8–9 *you would...you*   you would be more proud of this work than you are of all the usual acts of kindness that you perform.

10 *repent for doing good*   regret doing good.

13 *egall yoke*   equal bond.

14 *a like proportion*   a very close match.

15 *lineaments*   the features of the body, particularly the face.

17 *bosom lover*   best friend.

19–21 *How little...cruelty!*   I regard it as small expense to rescue someone so like Bassanio ('my soul') from such a desperate plight.

25 *husbandry...house*   the running of my household.

28 *contemplation*   meditation.

32 *abide*   stay.

33 *imposition*   task I have imposed (forced) on you.

34 *The which*   which.

How true a gentleman you send relief,
How dear a lover of my lord your husband,
I know you would be prouder of the work
Than customary bounty can enforce you.

PORTIA

I never did repent for doing good,   10
Nor shall not now; for in companions
That do converse and waste the time together,
Whose souls do bear an egall yoke of love,
There must be needs a like proportion
Of lineaments, of manners, and of spirit;   15
Which makes me think that this Antonio,
Being the bosom lover of my lord,
Must needs be like my lord. If it be so,
How little is the cost I have bestowed
In purchasing the semblance of my soul   20
From out the state of hellish cruelty! –
This comes too near the praising of myself;
Therefore no more of it; hear other things. –
Lorenzo, I commit into your hands
The husbandry and manage of my house,   25
Until my lord's return. For mine own part,
I have toward heaven breathed a secret vow
To live in prayer and contemplation,
Only attended by Nerissa here,
Until her husband and my lord's return.   30
There is a monastery two miles off,
And there we will abide. I do desire you
Not to deny this imposition,
The which my love and some necessity
Now lays upon you.

37 *My people*   my household.

38 *acknowledge*   obey.

48 *all th'endeavour of a man*   all the effort that a man can produce.

49 *Padua*   Italian city in north-east Italy, famous for its university.

51 *look what*   see what.

52 *imagined speed*   imaginable speed, i.e. as fast as possible.

53 *traject*   ferry.

56 *convenient*   appropriate, proper.

LORENZO

     Madam, with all my heart, 35
I shall obey you in all fair commands.

PORTIA

My people do already know my mind,
And will acknowledge you and Jessica
In place of Lord Bassanio and myself.
So fare you well till we shall meet again. 40

LORENZO

Fair thoughts and happy hours attend on you!

JESSICA

I wish your ladyship all heart's content.

PORTIA

I thank you for your wish, and am well pleased
To wish it back on you; fare you well, Jessica.

        Exeunt JESSICA *and* LORENZO

Now Balthazar, 45
As I have ever found thee honest-true,
So let me find thee still. Take this same letter,
And use thou all th' endeavour of a man
In speed to Padua. See thou render this
Into my cousin's hand, Doctor Bellario, 50
And look what notes and garments he doth give
  thee.
Bring them, I pray thee, with imagined speed
Unto the traject, to the common ferry
Which trades to Venice; waste no time in words,
But get thee gone! I shall be there before thee. 55

BALTHAZAR

Madam, I go with all convenient speed.

            Exit

60 *such a habit*   in such clothes.

61–2 *we are accomplished With that we lack*   we have what we lack, i.e. a man's body.

62 *wager*   bet.

63 *accoutered*   fitted out, dressed up.

65 *braver grace*   more panache, more style.

66 *speak...boy*   as if my voice was breaking.

67 *reed voice*   squeaky voice.

mincing   dainty.

68 *frays*   fights.

69 *bragging*   boastful.

quaint   clever, skilful.

71 *I denying*   I refused (to give my love).

72 *I could not do withal*   I could not help it.

74 *puny*   small, weak.

75–6 *I have...twelvemonth*   I left school over a year ago.

77 *Jacks*   lads.

80 *If thou...interpreter*   if you had been with anyone who would have taken that question obscenely. Nerissa's question ('Why, shall we turn to men?') means, of course, are we going to disguise ourselves as men? But it could have meant are we going to go out and find ourselves lovers?

81 *my whole device*   my whole plan.

PORTIA

Come on, Nerissa, I have work in hand
That you yet know not of; we'll see our husbands
Before they think of us!

NERISSA

Shall they see us?

PORTIA

They shall, Nerissa, but in such a habit   60
That they shall think we are accomplished
With that we lack. I'll hold thee any wager,
When we are both accoutered like young men,
I'll prove the prettier fellow of the two,
And wear my dagger with the braver grace,   65
And speak between the change of man and boy,
With a reed voice, and turn two mincing steps
Into a manly stride, and speak of frays
Like a fine bragging youth; and tell quaint lies
How honourable ladies sought my love,   70
Which I denying, they fell sick and died.
I could not do withal. Then I'll repent.
And wish, for all that, that I had not killed them.
And twenty of these puny lies I'll tell,
That men shall swear I have discontinued school   75
Above a twelvemonth. I have within my mind
A thousand·raw tricks of these bragging Jacks
Which I will practise.

NERISSA

Why, shall we turn to men?

PORTIA

Fie! what a question's that,
If thou wert near a lewd interpreter!   80
But come, I'll tell thee all my whole device

82 *stays for us*   waits for us.

84 *must measure*   must travel.

1–2 *the sins...children*   see Exodus 20:5.

3 *fear you*   am afraid for you.

plain with you   honest with you.

4 *agitation of the matter*   he means cogitation; his thoughts on the matter.

7 *neither*   only.

9 *Marry*   by the Virgin Mary; a mild swear word.

9–10 *got you not*   is not responsible for your birth, i.e. is not your real father.

11–12 *so the sins...visited upon me*   this way I will be punished for my mother's sins (rather than my father's).

14–15 *thus when I shun...mother*   according to the Greek poet Homer, Scylla and Charybdis were two perils that sailors faced. Scylla was a sea monster and Charybdis was a whirlpool. Sailors who tried to avoid one were often destroyed by the other.

15–16 *you are gone both ways*   either way you are damned.

When I am in my coach, which stays for us
At the park gate; and therefore haste away,
For we must measure twenty miles to-day.

Exeunt

Scene five

Belmont. The garden.

Enter LAUNCELOT *and* JESSICA.

LAUNCELOT
Yes, truly; for look you, the sins of the father are to
be laid upon the children; therefore, I promise you,
I fear you. I was always plain with you, and so now
I speak my agitation of the matter; therefore be of
good cheer, for truly I think you are damned. There   5
is but one hope in it that can do you any good, and
that is but a kind of bastard hope neither.

JESSICA
And what hope is that, I pray thee?

LAUNCELOT
Marry, you may partly hope that your father got
you not, that you are not the Jew's daughter.   10

JESSICA
That were a kind of bastard hope indeed; – so the
sins of my mother should be visited upon me.

LAUNCELOT
Truly, then I fear you are damned both by father
and mother; thus when I shun Scylla, your father, I
fall into Charybdis, your mother; well, you are gone   15
both ways.

20 *enow*   enough.

20–1 *e'en...another*   just as many as could live happily together.

21–2 *raise the price of hogs*   because Christians eat pigs ('hogs') and Jews do not.

23 *coals*   fire.

30 *are out*   are at odds, do not agree.

32–3 *commonwealth*   state.

36 *the getting up*   making pregnant.

35–6 *I shall answer...belly*   I shall have a better answer for my actions than you shall have for yours.

36 *the Moor*   presumably a servant in Portia's household.

38 *more than reason*   larger than she should be.

JESSICA

I shall be saved by my husband; he hath made me a
Christian!

LAUNCELOT

Truly, the more to blame he; we were Christians
enow before, e'en as many as could well live one by 20
another. This making of Christians will raise the
price of hogs – if we grow all to be pork-eaters, we
shall not shortly have a rasher on the coals for
money.

Enter LORENZO.

JESSICA

I'll tell my husband, Launcelot, what you say; here 25
he comes!

LORENZO

I shall grow jealous of you shortly, Launcelot, if you
thus get my wife into corners!

JESSICA

Nay, you need not fear us, Lorenzo; Launcelot and
I are out. He tells me flatly there's no mercy for me 30
in heaven, because I am a Jew's daughter; and he
says you are no good member of the commonwealth, for in converting Jews to Christians you
raise the price of pork.

LORENZO

I shall answer that better to the commonwealth than 35
you can the getting up of the negro's belly; the Moor
is with child by you, Launcelot!

LAUNCELOT

It is much that the Moor should be more than reason;

41-4 *the best grace...parrots*   the most intelligent thing to do will be to remain si█
and leave all the talking to the parrots, i.e. people like Launcelot who repeat w█
they have heard but get their words mixed up and do not, in any case,
understand what they are saying.

45 *they...stomachs*   they are all hungry.

48 *"cover" is the word*   they only need to be told to lay the table.

49 *Will you cover*   will you tell them to do so. Launcelot takes this as meaning w█
he cover his head (put his hat on), which he refuses to do in the presence of
Lorenzo and Jessica.

51 *quarrelling with occasion*   taking every opportunity to argue.

57 *it shall be covered*   the meat will be served in a dish with a cover on it.

58-9 *humours...govern*   as the mood takes you.

but if she be less than an honest woman, she is indeed
more than I took her for.   40

LORENZO

How every fool can play upon the word! I think the
best grace of wit will shortly turn into silence, and
discourse grow commendable in none only but parrots. – Go in, sirrah; bid them prepare for dinner!

LAUNCELOT

That is done, sir; they have all stomachs!   45

LORENZO

Goodly Lord, what a wit-snapper are you! then bid
them prepare dinner!

LAUNCELOT

That is done too, sir, only "cover" is the word.

LORENZO

Will you cover then, sir?

LAUNCELOT

Not so, sir, neither; I know my duty.   50

LORENZO

Yet more quarrelling with occasion! Wilt thou show
the whole wealth of thy wit in an instant? I pray
thee understand a plain man in his plain meaning:
go to thy fellows, bid them cover the table, serve in
the meat, and we will come in to dinner.   55

LAUNCELOT

For the table, sir, it shall be served in; for the meat,
sir, it shall be covered. For your coming in to dinner, sir, why, let it be as humours and conceits shall
govern.

Exit

60 *O dear discretion*   O such fine distinctions!
    suited   twisted.

63 *A many*   many.
    stand in better place   have a better job.

64 *Garnished*   dressed.

64–5 *that for...matter*   for the sake of word play fail to make any sense.

65 *How cheer'st thou*   are you happy?

68 *Past all expressing*   beyond my ability to say.

69 *live an upright life*   leads a good life (without sin).

72–3 *if on earth...heaven*   if he does not deserve the heaven he has found here on earth (with Portia) then he certainly will not deserve the real heaven.

74 *match*   betting game.

77 *Pawned with*   bet with.

81 *anon*   shortly.

82 *have a stomach*   am in the mood to do so.

LORENZO

O dear discretion, how his words are suited!   60
The fool hath planted in his memory
An army of good words, and I do know
A many fools that stand in better place,
Garnished like him, that for a tricksy word
Defy the matter. How cheer'st thou, Jessica?   65
And now, good sweet, say thy opinion,
How dost thou like the Lord Bassanio's wife?

JESSICA

Past all expressing; it is very meet
The Lord Bassanio live an upright life
For, having such a blessing in his lady,   70
He finds the joys of heaven here on earth,
And if on earth he do not merit it,
In reason he should never come to heaven!
Why, if two gods should play some heavenly match,
And on the wager lay two earthly women,   75
And Portia one, there must be something else
Pawned with the other, for the poor rude world
Hath not her fellow.

LORENZO

               Even such a husband
Hast thou of me, as she is for a wife.

JESSICA

Nay, but ask my opinion too of that.   80

LORENZO

I will anon; first, let us go to dinner.

JESSICA

Nay, let me praise you while I have a stomach.

84–5 *howsome'er...digest it* however you praise me I'll be able to accept it ('digest it') together with my dinner.

85 *set you forth* praise you at length. The phrase can also mean to set out a meal.

LORENZO

No, pray thee, let it serve for table-talk;
Then, howsome'er thou speak'st, 'mong other things
I shall digest it.

JESSICA

Well, I'll set you forth. 85

Exeunt

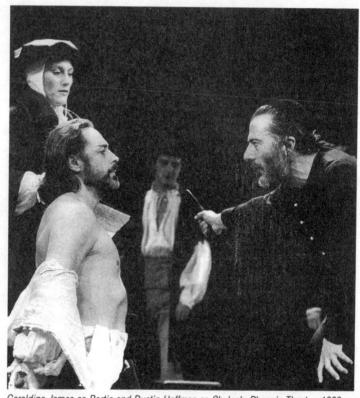

Geraldine James as Portia and Dustin Hoffman as Shylock: Pheonix Theatre, 1990 (Donald Cooper/Photostage).

Act 4: summary

Shylock demands that he be allowed to take his pound of flesh. No one, not even the Duke of Venice, can dissuade him and so the matter is brought to court. Unfortunately, Doctor Bellario cannot be present to defend Antonio. Instead he sends another young lawyer to represent him (Portia in disguise). Shylock is given the chance to take more than the money owed to him but he refuses, just as he refuses to listen to Portia's pleas for him to be merciful. He is jubilant when Portia finally appears to admit defeat and says that he may have his pound of flesh.

His happiness is short lived, however, as she quickly points out that he is not entitled to spill any of Antonio's blood and that he must cut an *exact* pound of flesh – conditions impossible to fulfil. She also adds that, as the conditions of the bond amount to an attempt on Antonio's life, Shylock's own life and goods are forfeit to the State of Venice. Shylock is allowed to live providing he agrees to meet certain conditions, amongst them being an agreement to become a Christian and to give half his goods to Antonio.

Shylock leaves the court a broken man, and Bassanio offers to reward the lawyer who has saved his friend. Portia refuses to accept anything except the ring that she gave him, which Bassanio has promised not to part with. Swayed by Antonio's pleas Bassanio sends the ring after Portia once she has left. Similarly Gratiano gives his ring to the disguised Nerissa.

4 *A stony adversary*   an enemy without any feelings.

5 *Uncapable of*   not able to feel.

  void   empty, without substance.

6 *dram*   drop.

7–8 *to qualify His rigorous course*   alter (for the better) the harsh punishment that he insists upon.

8 *stands obdurate*   remains unmoved.

10 *Out of his envy's reach*   out of reach of his hatred and malice.

13 *tyranny*   violence.

Act Four

Scene one

Venice. A Court of Justice.

Enter the DUKE, *the Magnificoes* ANTONIO, BASSANIO, *and* GRATIANO, SALERIO *and others.*

DUKE
What, is Antonio here?

ANTONIO
Ready, so please your grace!

DUKE
I am sorry for thee; thou art come to answer
A stony adversary, an inhuman wretch,
Uncapable of pity, void and empty   5
From any dram of mercy.

ANTONIO
                              I have heard
Your grace hath ta'en great pains to qualify
His rigorous course; but since he stands obdurate,
And that no lawful means can carry me
Out of his envy's reach, I do oppose   10
My patience to his fury, and am armed
To suffer with a quietness of spirit
The very tyranny and rage of his.

DUKE
Go, one, call the Jew into the court.

SALERIO
He is ready at the door; he comes, my lord.   15

18 *but leadest this fashion*   are only continuing with this outward show.

19 *To the last hour of act*   to the last moment.

20 *more strange*   more extraordinary.

24 *loose the forfeiture*   give up your demands (for Antonio's flesh).

26 *Forgive...principal*   agree not to demand all of the money actually lent to Antonio. The suggestion is that Shylock will not insist on the interest being paid.

29 *Enow*   enough.

31 *From brassy...flint*   two different ways of saying hardhearted; brass and flint both being renowned for their hardness.

32 *Turks, and Tartars*   non-Christian people and, therefore, the Duke suggests, not people who value qualities like mercy and forgiveness.

33 *offices*   deeds.

34 *a gentle answer*   a pun on the word Gentile (meaning non-Jew). It is not the first time that this pun has been used.

35 *possessed*   told.

36 *Sabbath*   the Jewish holy day which begins on Friday evening and takes in all of Saturday.

37 *the due*   the money due to me.

39 *your charter...freedom*   the system by which the State of Venice makes and upholds its own laws.

41 *carrion flesh*   rotting meat.

43 *it is my humour*   it pleases me. The implication here is that there is no rational, logical reason for Shylock's desire.

Enter SHYLOCK.

DUKE

Make room, and let him stand before our face.
Shylock, the world thinks, and I think so too,
That thou but leadest this fashion of thy malice
To the last hour of act, and then 't is thought
Thou'lt show thy mercy and remorse, more strange   20
Than is thy strange apparent cruelty;
And where thou now exact'st the penalty,
Which is a pound of this poor merchant's flesh,
Thou wilt not only loose the forfeiture,
But, touched with human gentleness and love,   25
Forgive a moiety of the principal,
Glancing an eye of pity on his losses
That have of late so huddled on his back
Enow to press a royal merchant down,
And pluck commiseration of his state   30
From brassy bosoms and rough hearts of flint,
From stubborn Turks, and Tartars never trained
To offices of tender courtesy.
We all expect a gentle answer, Jew!

SHYLOCK

I have possessed your grace of what I purpose,   35
And by our holy Sabbath have I sworn
To have the due and forfeit of my bond.
If you deny it, let the danger light
Upon your charter and your city's freedom!
You'll ask me why I rather choose to have   40
A weight of carrion flesh than to receive
Three thousand ducats. I'll not answer that!
But say it is my humour – is it answered?
What if my house be troubled with a rat,
And I be pleased to give ten thousand ducats   45

46 *baned*   poisoned.

47 *gaping pig*   when a whole roasted pig's head was served at table it often had some kind of fruit placed in the open ('gaping') mouth as decoration. Shylock, as a Jew, would not eat pork.

49 *sings i' the' nose*   a high pitched, nasal sound.

50–2 *for affection...loathes*   the body's desires control its emotions, and so dictate the way in which the body reacts to things these desires either like or dislike.

53 *no firm reason...rendered*   no fixed, right answer to be given.

60 *a lodged hate*   a hatred that is immovable.

62 *A losing suit*   a case that cannot be won because Shylock will not get his money back.

64 *current*   the way in which Shylock's cruelty is moving.

67 *Hates...kill?*   would any man consider letting something that he hates live?

To have it baned? – what, are you answered yet?
Some men there are love not a gaping pig;
Some that are mad if they behold a cat;
And others, when the bagpipe sings i' the' nose,
Cannot contain their urine – for affection,   50
Master of passion, sways it to the mood
Of what it likes or loathes. Now for your answer:
As there is no firm reason to be rendered
Why *he* cannot abide a gaping pig,
Why *he* a harmless, necessary cat,   55
Why *he* a woollen bagpipe, but of force
Must yield to such inevitable shame
As to offend, himself being offended;
So can I give no reason, nor I will not,
More than a lodged hate and a certain loathing   60
I bear Antonio, that I follow thus
A losing suit against him! – Are you answered?

BASSANIO
This is no answer, thou unfeeling man,
To excuse the current of thy cruelty.

SHYLOCK
I am not bound to please thee with my answers!   65

BASSANIO
Do all men kill the things they do not love?

SHYLOCK
Hates any man the thing he would not kill?

BASSANIO
Every offence is not a hate at first!

SHYLOCK
What! wouldst thou have à serpent sting thee twice?

181

70 *think you*   consider the fact that you.

72 *bid...height*   tell the high tide not to come so far up the beach.

77 *fretten*   blown about.

82 *all brief...conveniency*   Antonio wants everything over as quickly and clearly as possible.

92 *in abject...parts*   to carry out those kinds of tasks only suitable for slaves.

95 *burthens*   burdens.

96–7 *let their palates...viands*   let them eat the same kind of foods as you.

ANTONIO

I pray you think you question with the Jew.   70
You may as well go stand upon the beach
And bid the main flood bate his usual height;
You may as well use question with the wolf,
Why he hath made the ewe bleat for the lamb;
You may as well forbid the mountain pines   75
To wag their high tops, and to make no noise
When they are fretten with the gusts of heaven;
You may as well do anything most hard
As seek to soften that – than which what's harder? –
His Jewish heart! Therefore, I do beseech you,   80
Make no more offers, use no farther means,
But with all brief and plain conveniency
Let me have judgement, and the Jew his will!

BASSANIO

For thy three thousand ducats, here is six!

SHYLOCK

If every ducat in six thousand ducats   85
Were in six parts, and every part a ducat,
I would not draw them; I would have my bond!

DUKE

How shalt thou hope for mercy, rendering none?

SHYLOCK

What judgement shall I dread, doing no wrong?
You have among you many a purchased slave,   90
Which, like your asses, and your dogs and mules,
You use in abject and in slavish parts,
Because you bought them; shall I say to you,
Let them be free, marry them to your heirs?
Why sweat they under burthens? let their beds   95
Be made as soft as yours, and let their palates

183

102   *no force...Venice*   the laws of Venice have no power.

104   *Upon my power*   it is within my powers.

106   *to determine this*   to try this case.

107   *here stays without*   there is waiting outside.

114   *tainted wether*   sick sheep.

115   *Meetest for death*   fit only for death.

118   *epitaph*   words to be said or written down after death, summing up the dead
        person's life.

Be seasoned with such viands? You will answer
"The slaves are ours." – So do I answer you:
The pound of flesh which I demand of him
Is dearly bought, 't is mine and I will have it;   100
If you deny me, fie upon your law!
There is no force in the decrees of Venice!
I stand for judgement; answer, shall I have it?

DUKE

Upon my power I may dismiss this court,
Unless Bellario, a learned doctor,   105
Whom I have sent for to determine this,
Come here to-day.

SALERIO

          My lord, here stays without
A messenger with letters from the doctor,
New come from Padua.

DUKE

Bring us the letters! call the messenger!   110

BASSANIO

Good cheer, Antonio! what, man, courage yet!
The Jew shall have my flesh, blood, bones and all,
Ere thou shalt lose for me one drop of blood.

ANTONIO

I am a tainted wether of the flock,
Meetest for death; the weakest kind of fruit   115
Drops earliest to the ground, and so let me;
You cannot better be employed, Bassanio,
Than to live still and write mine epitaph.

Enter NERISSA, *dressed like a lawyer's clerk.*

DUKE

Came you from Padua, from Bellario?

185

121 *whet*   sharpen. Shylock is sharpening the knife on the sole of his shoe, hence the pun that follows.

122 *the forfeiture*   that which you agreed to give up (i.e. Antonio's pound of flesh).

124 *keen*   sharp.

125 *bear half...envy*   the sharpest metal (an executioner's axe) is still not as sharp as Shylock's hatred.

127 *wit*   intelligence.

128 *inexorable*   immovable.

129 *for they life...accused*   there is no justice whilst you live.

130–1 *Thou almost...Pythagoras*   Gratiano says that he is almost tempted to give up his Christian faith and believe in the ideas of Pythagoras. Pythagoras was a philosopher who taught that the souls of men went (transmigrated) into other bodies when they died.

132 *infuse*   seep into.

133 *trunks*   bodies.

currish   dog-like.

135 *fell*   evil.

fleet   move swiftly away.

136 *unhallowed dam*   cursed mother.

139–40 *Till thou...loud*   unless you can detach the seal from the bond (see note to Act 1, scene 3, line 140) by talking so loudly, you are wearing out your voice.

142 *cureless ruin*   spoilt passed the point of repair.

NERISSA

From both, my lord. Bellario greets your grace.   120

She gives him a letter.

BASSANIO

Why dost thou whet thy knife so earnestly?

SHYLOCK

To cut the forfeiture from that bankrupt there!

GRATIANO

Not on thy sole, but on thy soul, harsh Jew,
Thou mak'st thy knife keen; but no metal can,
No, not the hangman's axe, bear half the keenness 125
Of thy sharp envy. Can no prayers pierce thee?

SHYLOCK

No, none that *thou* hast wit enough to make.

GRATIANO

O, be thou damned, inexorable dog!
And for thy life let justice be accused;
Thou almost mak'st me waver in my faith   130
To hold opinion with Pythagoras,
That souls of animals infuse themselves
Into the trunks of men: thy currish spirit
Governed a wolf, who, hanged for human slaughter,
Even from the gallows did his fell soul fleet,   135
And, whilst thou layest in thy unhallowed dam,
Infused itself in thee; for thy desires
Are wolvish, bloody, starved, and ravenous.

SHYLOCK

Till thou canst rail the seal from off my bond,
Thou but offend'st thy lungs to speak so loud;   140
Repair thy wit, good youth, or it will fall
To cureless ruin. I stand here for law.

187

143 *doth commend*   does recommend.

145 *hard by*   close at hand.

148 *courteous conduct*   guide him politely.

154 *cause in controversy*   the issue in dispute.

155–6 *furnished with my opinion*   he knows my views.

158 *importunity*   unavailability, due to illness.

   to fill up...stead   to take my place in helping your Grace.

159–60 *to let him lack...estimation*   do not let his youth make people underestimate his abilities.

162 *whose trial...commendation*   if you accept his help it will become obvious why I have recommended him.

DUKE

This letter from Bellario doth commend
A young and learned doctor to our court.
Where is he?

NERISSA

He attendeth here hard by   145
To know your answer, whether you'll admit him.

DUKE

With all my heart; some three or four of you
Go give him courteous conduct to this place;
Meantime the court shall hear Bellario's letter.
(*Reads*) *Your grace shall understand that at the receipt of* 150
your letter I am very sick, but in the instant that your messen-
ger came, in loving visitation was with me a young doctor of
Rome; his name is Balthazar. I acquainted him with the
cause in controversy between the Jew and Antonio the mer-
chant; we turned o'er many books together; he is furnished 155
with my opinion, which, bettered with his own learning, the
greatness whereof I cannot enough commend, comes with him
at my importunity, to fill up your grace's request in my stead.
I beseech you let his lack of years be no impediment to let him
lack a reverend estimation, for I never knew so young a body 160
with so old a head. I leave him to your gracious acceptance,
whose trial shall better publish his commendation.

Enter PORTIA, *dressed as* BALTHAZAR, *a doctor of laws.*

You hear the learn'd Bellario what he writes,
(*He sees* PORTIA) And here, I take it, is the doctor
   come.
(*To* PORTIA) Give me your hand. Came you from old
   Bellario?   165

PORTIA

I did, my lord.

167–8 *Are you...court?*   are you familiar with the details of this case that we are here to try?

174–5 *in such rule...proceed*   your case has been followed so correctly that Venetian law cannot stop you if you continue like this.

176 *You stand within his danger*   you are at risk from him.

177 *confess the bond*   admit to having made the agreement.

178 *must*   Portia means here that Shylock as a matter of humanity will just have to be merciful. Shylock, however, misinterprets this as meaning that he has no choice in the matter.

179 *On what compulsion must I*   what is there to make me?

DUKE

You are welcome; take your place;
Are you acquainted with the difference
That holds this present question in the court?

PORTIA

I am informèd throughly of the cause.
Which is the merchant here? and which the Jew?　170

DUKE

Antonio and old Shylock, both stand forth.

PORTIA

Is your name Shylock?

SHYLOCK

Shylock is my name.

PORTIA

Of a strange nature is the suit you follow,
Yet in such rule that the Venetian law
Cannot impugn you as you do proceed.　　　175
(To ANTONIO) You stand within his danger, do you
　　not?

ANTONIO

Ay, so he says.

PORTIA

Do you confess the bond?

ANTONIO

I do.

PORTIA

Then must the Jew be merciful.

SHYLOCK

On what compulsion must I? tell me that.

191

180   *strained*   constrained. In other words, nothing can compel or force mercy, it has to arise naturally.

184   *'T is mightiest...mightiest*   it is at its strongest when it is a quality shown by those in power.

      becomes   suits.

186–7   *His sceptre...majesty*   the sceptre (ornamental rod) held by kings is a symbol of their earthly ('temporal') power, and it is this power that prompts the feelings of awe and respect that people have for kings.

189   *sway*   rule.

191   *It is an attribute to God*   it is a God-like quality.

192   *show likest*   appear most similar to.

193   *seasons*   goes with, flavours.

195–6   *That in the course...salvation*   if we only received justice then none of us would be saved from going to Hell (because we are all guilty of sin).

197   *And that same prayer*   the Lord's prayer which contains the lines: 'forgive us our trespasses, as we forgive those who trespass against us'.

      render   do.

199   *mitigate*   moderate, reduce.

201   *Must needs*   will have to.

202   *My deeds upon my head!*   I will accept the consequences of my own actions.

      crave   want, desire.

204   *discharge*   pay back

205   *tender*   offer in payment.

PORTIA

> The quality of mercy is not strained; 180
> It droppeth as the gentle rain from heaven
> Upon the place beneath; it is twice blest:
> It blesseth him that gives, and him that takes;
> 'T is mightiest in the mightiest; it becomes
> The thronèd monarch better than his crown. 185
> His sceptre shows the force of temporal power,
> The attribute to awe and majesty,
> Wherein doth sit the dread and fear of kings;
> But mercy is above this sceptred sway;
> It is enthronèd in the nearts of kings; 190
> It is an attribute to God himself;
> And earthly power doth then show likest God's
> When mercy seasons justice. Therefore, Jew,
> Though justice be thy plea, consider this,
> That in the course of justice none of us 195
> Should see salvation; we do pray for mercy,
> And that same prayer doth teach us all to render
> The deeds of mercy. I have spoke thus much
> To mitigate the justice of thy plea,
> Which, if thou follow, this strict court of Venice 200
> Must needs give sentence 'gainst the merchant there.

SHYLOCK

> My deeds upon my head! I crave the law,
> The penalty and forfeit of my bond.

PORTIA

> Is he not able to discharge the money?

BASSANIO

> Yes, here I tender it for him in the court; 205
> Yea, twice the sum; if that will not suffice,

209–10 *it must appear...truth*   it seems that evil (Shylock's hatred) has overcome what should rightfully happen.

211 *Wrest...authority*   just for once use your power to bend the law.

212 *To do...wrong*   bending the law is seen by Bassanio as being a lesser evil than letting Shylock win this case.

213 *curb*   hold back.

216 *'T will be...precedent*   if this is done once it will be used as an example when judging similar cases.

217–8 *many an error...state*   if this case is used as an example then there will be mistakes made when cases are tried in the future.

219 *Daniel*   a young prophet who successfully tried a seemingly hopeless case in the Bible. For the full story see the Apocrypha.

225 *perjury*   to lie after having sworn to tell the truth.

I will be bound to pay it ten times o'er
On forfeit of my hands, my head, my heart;
If this will not suffice, it must appear
That malice bears down truth. And I beseech you 210
Wrest once the law to your authority;
To do a great right, do a little wrong,
And curb this cruel devil of his will.

PORTIA

It must not be; there is no power in Venice
Can alter a decree establishèd; 215
'T will be recorded for a precedent,
And many an error by the same example
Will rush into the state. It cannot be:

SHYLOCK

A Daniel come to judgement! yea, a Daniel!
O wise young judge, how I do honour thee! 220

PORTIA

I pray you let me look upon the bond.

SHYLOCK

Here 't is, most reverend doctor, here it is.

PORTIA

Shylock, there's thrice thy money offered thee.

SHYLOCK

An oath, an oath, I have an oath in heaven. –
Shall I lay perjury upon my soul? 225
No, not for Venice.

PORTIA

          Why, this bond is forfeit,
And lawfully by this the Jew may claim
A pound of flesh, to be by him cut off

230 *tear the bond*   tear up the paper on which the agreement has been written.

231 *tenor*   terms set out in the bond.

233–4 *your exposition...sound*   your explanation of the legal position has been without fault.

234 *I charge you*   I command you.

235 *you are a well-deserving pillar*   you hold an important place in seeing that the law is correctly observed.

238 *To alter me*   to make me change my mind.

I stay here   I maintain my position, I have not changed my mind.

243–4 *For the intent...penalty*   everything in the law logically dictates the penalty.

Nearest the merchant's heart. (*To* SHYLOCK) Be
   merciful,
Take thrice thy money; bid me tear the bond.   230

SHYLOCK

When it is paid, according to the tenor.
It doth appear you are a worthy judge,
You know the law; your exposition
Hath been most sound. I charge you by the law,
Whereof you are a well-deserving pillar,   235
Proceed to judgement; by my soul I swear,
There is no power in the tongue of man
To alter me. I stay here on my bond.

ANTONIO

Most heartily I do beseech the court
To give the judgement.

PORTIA

                  Why then thus it is: 240
You must prepare your bosom for his knife.

SHYLOCK

O noble judge! O excellent young man!

PORTIA

For the intent and purpose of the law
Hath full relation to the penalty,
Which here appeareth due upon the bond.   245

SHYLOCK

'T is very true. O wise and upright judge,
How much more elder art thou than thy looks!

PORTIA

(*To* ANTONIO) Therefore, lay bare your bosom.

251 *balance* scales.

253 *on your charge* at your cost. Shylock is expected to pay the doctor's fees.

255 *nominated* stated.

260 *armed* ready.

264 *her use* Fortune's way.

SHYLOCK

                         Ay, his breast,
So says the bond, doth it not, noble judge?
"Nearest his heart", those are the very words.   250

PORTIA

It is so. Are there balance here to weigh
The flesh?

SHYLOCK

          I have them ready.

PORTIA

Have by some surgeon, Shylock, on your charge,
To stop his wounds, lest he do bleed to death.

SHYLOCK

Is it so nominated in the bond?   255

PORTIA

It is not so expressed, but what of that?
'T were good you do so much for charity.

SHYLOCK

I cannot find it; 't is not in the bond.

PORTIA

(*To* ANTONIO) You merchant, have you anything to
    say?

ANTONIO

But little. I am armed and well prepared.   260
Give me your hand, Bassanio; fare you well,
Grieve not that I am fall'n to this for you,
For herein Fortune shows herself more kind
Than is her custom. It is still her use
To let the wretched man outlive this wealth,   265
To view with hollow eye and wrinkled brow

267 *penance*   punishment undertaken to show sorrow for sinning.

270 *process*   what happened.

274 *Repent but you*   if only you show that you are sorry to lose a friend, I will not b
sorry that I'm paying this debt.

281 *esteemed*   valued.

284–5 *Your wife...the offer*   Portia is saying 'your wife wouldn't thank you for saying
that if she were here'. Of course she is here, because Portia, disguised as
Balthazar, is Bassanio's wife. Thus the audience knows something that the
character does not know; this is called *dramatic irony*.

286 *I protest*   I promise.

An age of poverty: from which ling'ring penance
Of such misery doth she cut me off.
Commend me to your honourable wife;
Tell her the process of Antonio's end, 270
Say how I loved you, speak me fair in death;
And when the tale is told, bid her be judge
Whether Bassanio had not once a love;
Repent but you that you shall lose your friend
And he repents not that he pays your debt. 275
For if the Jew do cut but deep enough,
I'll pay it instantly, with all my heart.

BASSANIO

Antonio, I am married to a wife
Which is as dear to me as life itself,
But life itself, my wife, and all the world, 280
Are not with me esteemed above thy life.
I would lose all, ay, sacrifice them all
Here to this devil, to deliver you.

PORTIA

Your wife would give you little thanks for that
If she were by to hear you make the offer. 285

GRATIANO

I have a wife who I protest I love –
I would she were in heaven, so she could
Entreat some power to change this currish Jew.

NERISSA

'T is well you offer it behind her back;
The wish would make else an unquiet house. 290

SHYLOCK (*Aside*)

These be the Christian husbands! I have a
daughter –

292   *stock of Barabbas*   Barabbas was the Jewish criminal set free instead of Chris
        Shylock wishes that Jessica had married any Jew (no matter how bad) rather
        than the Christian Lorenzo.

294   *trifle time*   waste time.

301   *Tarry a little*   wait a moment.

302   *no jot*   no drop.

307–8   *confiscate Unto*   confiscated by.

310   *the act*   the law that states these conditions.

Would any of the stock of Barabbas
Had been her husband, rather than a Christian.
(*Aloud*) We trifle time; I pray thee pursue sentence.

PORTIA

A pound of that same merchant's flesh is thine;   295
The court awards it, and the law doth give it.

SHYLOCK

Most rightful judge!

PORTIA

And you must cut this flesh from off his breast;
The law allows it, and the court awards it.

SHYLOCK

Most learned judge! A sentence! Come, prepare!   300

PORTIA

Tarry a little; there is something else:
This bond doth give thee here no jot of blood;
The words expressly are "a pound of flesh";
Take then thy bond, take thou thy pound of flesh,
But in the cutting it, if thou dost shed   305
One drop of Christian blood, thy lands and goods
Are (by the laws of Venice) confiscate
Unto the state of Venice.

GRATIANO

                              O upright judge! –
Mark, Jew – O learned judge!

SHYLOCK

Is that the law?

PORTIA

                              Thyself shalt see the act;   310
For as thou urgest justice, be assured

316 *Soft* wait.

323–6 *be it but...poor scruple* a scruple is a unit of weight used by chemists and is made up of twenty grains. Shylock is being told that he must be impossibly accurate when cutting the pound of flesh.

330 *on the hip* see note to Act 1, scene 3, line 42.

Thou shalt have justice more than thou desir'st.

GRATIANO

O learned judge! – Mark, Jew, a learned judge!

SHYLOCK

I take this offer then; pay the bond thrice,
And let the Christian go.

BASSANIO

                Here is the money.   315

PORTIA

Soft!
The Jew shall have all justice; soft, no haste!
He shall have nothing but the penalty.

GRATIANO

O Jew! an upright judge, a learned judge!

PORTIA

Therefore prepare thee to cut off the flesh;   320
Shed thou no blood, nor cut thou less nor more
But just a pound of flesh. If thou tak'st more
Or less than a just pound, be it but so much
As makes it light or heavy in the substance
Or the division of the twentieth part   325
Of one poor scruple – nay, if the scale do turn
But in the estimation of a hair,
Thou diest, and all thy goods are confiscate.

GRATIANO

A second Daniel, A Daniel, Jew! –
Now, infidel, I have you on the hip.   330

PORTIA

Why doth the Jew pause? (*To* SHYLOCK) Take thy
   forfeiture.

332 *my principal*   the sum of money that Shylock began with.

338 *barely*   only (without any interest added to it).

342 *I'll stay no longer question*   I will not stay to continue this case any further.

344 *enacted*   set out.

345 *an alien*   i.e. not a citizen of Venice.

348 *The party...contrive*   the person against whom he has plotted.

350 *privy coffer*   the Duke's (as opposed to the State's) treasury.

352 *'gainst all other voice*   regardless of what anyone else has to say.

SHYLOCK

Give me my principal, and let me go.

BASSANIO

I have it ready for thee; here it is.

PORTIA

He hath refused it in the open court;
He shall have merely justice and his bond.   335

GRATIANO

A Daniel still say I, a second Daniel!
I thank thee Jew for teaching me that word.

SHYLOCK

Shall I not have barely my principal?

PORTIA

Thou shalt have nothing but the forfeiture,
To be so taken at thy peril, Jew.   340

SHYLOCK

Why then, the devil give him good of it;
I'll stay no longer question.

PORTIA

                         Tarry, Jew;
The law hath yet another hold on you.
It is enacted in the laws of Venice,
If it be proved against an alien   345
That by direct or indirect attempts
He seek the life of any citizen,
The party 'gainst the which he doth contrive,
Shall seize one half his goods; the other half
Comes to the privy coffer of the state,   350
And the offender's life lies in the mercy
Of the Duke only, 'gainst all other voice.

353 *predicament* awkward situation.

354 *by manifest proceeding* by everything you have done.

356 *contrived* plotted.

357–8 *thou hast incurred...rehearsed* you have brought down upon yourself the penalty that I have just explained.

359 *Down* down on your knees.

362 *cord* a rope to hang oneself with.

358 *Which humbleness...fine* if you accept this humbly I might insist on merely a fine rather than half of all you own.

369 *for the state, not for Antonio* only reduce the State's half of all Shylock owns to a fine, the other half must go to Antonio intact.

371–2 *the prop...house* the one thing that holds my household together.

375 *A halter gratis* a hangman's noose, free of charge.

In which predicament I say thou stand'st;
For it appears by manifest proceeding,
That indirectly, and directly too,   355
Thou hast contrived against the very life
Of the defendant; and thou hast incurred
The danger formerly by me rehearsed.
Down, therefore, and beg mercy of the duke.

GRATIANO

Beg that thou may'st have leave to hang thyself.   360
And yet, thy wealth being forfeit to the state,
Thou hast not left the value of a cord;
Therefore thou must be hanged at the state's
    charge.

DUKE

That thou shalt see the difference of our spirit,
I pardon thee thy life before thou ask it;   365
For half thy wealth, it is Antonio's,
The other half comes to the general state,
Which humbleness may drive unto a fine.

PORTIA

Ay, for the state, not for Antonio.

SHYLOCK

Nay, take my life and all, pardon not that.   370
You take my house when you do take the prop
That doth sustain my house; you take my life
When you do take the means whereby I live.

PORTIA

What mercy can you render him, Antonio?

GRATIANO

A halter gratis; nothing else, for God's sake!   375

377 *To quit*   not to insist.

378 *so he*   as long as he.

379–81 *to render it...his daughter*   when he dies his money must be given to Lorenzo who has eloped with Shylock's daughter, Jessica.

384 *record a gift*   make a will.

387 *recant*   take back.

394 *in christening...godfathers*   a christening is the ceremony at which children are accepted into the Christian church. The godfathers would become protectors of the child. 'Godfather' was also a slang term for members of the jury, at a trial.

ANTONIO

So please my lord the Duke and all the court
To quit the fine for one half of his goods,
I am content; so he will let me have
The other half in use, to render it
Upon his death unto the gentleman   380
That lately stole his daughter.
Two things provided more, – that for this
    favour
He presently become a Christian;
The other, that he do record a gift,
Here in the court, of all he dies possessed   385
Unto his son Lorenzo and his daughter.

DUKE

He shall do this, or else I do recant
The pardon that I late pronouncèd here.

PORTIA

Art thou contented, Jew? What dost thou say?

SHYLOCK

I am content.

PORTIA

                    Clerk, draw a deed of gift.   390

SHYLOCK

I pray you give me leave to go from hence;
I am not well; send the deed after me,
And I will sign it.

DUKE

                    Get thee gone, but do it.

GRATIANO

In christening shalt thou have two godfathers;

211

395 *ten more* this would bring the number up to twelve, thus making up a jury who would have sentenced Shylock to death if Gratiano had had his way.

397 *entreat* beg.

398 *I humbly...pardon* I humbly ask your Grace to excuse me (from this invitation).

400 *meet* fitting.

401 *your leisure serves you not* you have so little time.

402 *gratify* reward.

403 *much bound to him* you owe him a lot.

406 *in lieu whereof* as a payment for this.

407–8 *Three thousand...withal* we will willingly reward you for your troubles with the 3000 ducats originally offered to Shylock.

414 *my mind...mercenary* I do not make a living out of hiring out my intellect.

415 *know me...again* recognise or acknowledge me when we meet again. This is an example of dramatic irony as the audience knows that this is Portia talking, but Antonio does not.

Had I been judge, thou shouldst have had ten more, 395
To bring thee to the gallows, not to the font.

Exit SHYLOCK

DUKE
Sir, I entreat you home with me to dinner.

PORTIA
I humbly do desire your grace of pardon;
I must away this night toward Padua,
And it is meet I presently set forth. 400

DUKE
I am sorry that your leisure serves you not.
Antonio, gratify this gentleman,
For in my mind you are much bound to him.

Exit DUKE *and his train*

BASSANIO
Most worthy gentleman, I and my friend
Have by your wisdom been this day acquitted 405
Of grievous penalties, in lieu whereof,
Three thousand ducats due unto the Jew
We freely cope your courteous pains withal.

ANTONIO
And stand indebted over and above
In love and service to you evermore. 410

PORTIA
He is well paid that is well satisfied,
And I, delivering you, am satisfied,
And therein do account myself well paid;
My mind was never yet more mercenary.
I pray you know me when we meet again; 415
I wish you well, and so I take my leave.

417   *of force*   I am compelled.

      attempt   try to persuade.

418   *as a tribute*   as a payment made out of gratitude.

421   *press me far*   you are very insistent.

429   *have a mind to it*   want to have it.

432   *find it out by proclamation*   discover where it (the most expensive ring) is to be found by announcing my search publicly.

433   *Only...pardon me*   as far as this ring is concerned, I beg you to free me from your demand.

434   *liberal in offers*   very generous when it comes to making offers (but not when it comes to carrying them out).

435–6   *You taught me...answered*   you wanted me to ask something of you, like a beggar, and now you treat me like a beggar by refusing my wish.

BASSANIO

Dear sir, of force I must attempt you further;
Take some remembrance of us as a tribute,
Not as a fee. Grant me two things, I pray you:
Not to deny me, and to pardon me.   420

PORTIA

You press me far, and therefore I will yield.
Give me your gloves; I'll wear them for your sake;
And, for your love, I'll take this ring from you.
Do not draw back your hand; I'll take no more,
And you in love shall not deny me this!   425

BASSANIO

This ring, good sir? Alas, it is a trifle;
I will not shame myself to give you this!

PORTIA

I will have nothing else but only this,
And now methinks I have a mind to it!

BASSANIO

There's more depends on this than on the value.   430
The dearest ring in Venice will I give you,
And find it out by proclamation,
Only for this I pray you pardon me!

PORTIA

I see, sir, you are liberal in offers;
You taught me first to beg, and now methinks   435
You teach me how a beggar should be answered.

BASSANIO

Good sir, this ring was given me by my wife,
And when she put it on, she made me vow
That I should neither sell, nor give, nor lose it.

440 *'scuse* excuse.

443 *hold out enemy* be your enemy.

451 *thither* go there.

453 *Fly* travel speedily.

1 *Inquire the Jew's house out* find out where Shylock ('the Jew') lives.

PORTIA

That 'scuse serves many men to save their gifts,   440
And if your wife be not a mad woman,
And know how well I have deserved this ring,
She would not hold out enemy for ever
For giving it to me. Well, peace be with you!

Exeunt PORTIA *and* NERISSA

ANTONIO

My Lord Bassanio, let him have the ring;   445
Let his deservings and my love withal
Be valued 'gainst your wife's commandement.

BASSANIO

Go, Gratiano, run and overtake him,
Give him the ring, and bring him if thou canst
Unto Antonio's house. Away, make haste.   450

Exit GRATIANO

Come, you and I will thither presently,
And in the morning early will we both
Fly toward Belmont. – Come, Antonio.

Exeunt

Scene two

Venice. A street.

Enter PORTIA *and* NERISSA.

PORTIA

Inquire the Jew's house out; give him this deed,
And let him sign it. We'll away to-night,
And be a day before our husbands home.
This deed will be well welcome to Lorenzo!

6 *advice* thought.

15 *I warrant* I bet.

old swearing much swearing.

17 *outface* be so self-confident that they will back down.

18 *tarry* wait.

Enter GRATIANO.

GRATIANO

Fair sir, you are well o'erta'en: 5
My Lord Bassanio, upon more advice
Hath sent you here this ring, and doth entreat
Your company at dinner.

PORTIA

That cannot be;
His ring I do accept most thankfully,
And so I pray you tell him. Furthermore,   10
I pray you show my youth old Shylock's house.

GRATIANO

That will I do.

NERISSA

Sir, I would speak with you.
(*Aside to* PORTIA) I'll see if I can get my husband's
    ring,
Which I did make him swear to keep for ever.

PORTIA

Thou may'st, I warrant. We shall have old
    swearing   15
That they did give the rings away to men;
But we'll outface them, and outswear them too.
Away, make haste! Thou know'st where I will tarry.

NERISSA

Come, good sir, will you show me to this house?

Exeunt

Lorenzo and Jessica: Royal Shakespeare Company, 1981 (Christopher Pearce/The Panic Pictures Library).

Act 5: summary

Portia and Nerissa arrive in Belmont moments before the arrival of Bassanio, Antonio and Gratiano. Portia pretends to be angry about the fact that Bassanio has given away her ring, and will not listen to his explanations. Bassanio promises faithfully never to break his word to her again, and Antonio, for the second time in the play, finds himself standing guarantor for his friend.

With all the characters reconciled the play ends happily as Portia reveals her part in the court case, and Antonio is told that three of his ships have survived after all and he is once again a wealthy man.

1 *In* on.

4–6 *Troilus . . . Cressid lay that night* one of the sons of King Priam of Troy and the lover of Cressida. Cressida was taken as a hostage by the Greeks in the Trojan War – hence the separation referred to here.

7 *Thisbe* the beloved of Pyramus. She fled from a prearranged meeting with her lover when she was frightened by a lion.

o'ertrip the dew step lightly across the dewy grass.

10 *Dido* Queen of Carthage and lover of Aeneas who deserted her.

11 *waft* wafted, waved.

13 *Medea* Medea helped Jason win the golden fleece and then eloped with him. Jason later abandoned her and married someone else.

Aeson Jason's father. Medea used her magical skills to heal him.

Act Five

Belmont. A green place in front of Portia's house. Night-time.

Enter LORENZO *and* JESSICA.

LORENZO

  The moon shines bright. In such a night as this,
  When the sweet wind did gently kiss the trees,
  And they did make no noise, in such a night
  Troilus methinks mounted the Trojan walls,
  And sighed his soul toward the Grecian tents   5
  Where Cressid lay that night.

JESSICA

                     In such a night
  Did Thisbe fearfully o'ertrip the dew,
  And saw the lion's shadow ere himself,
  And ran dismayed away.

LORENZO

                In such a night
  Stood Dido with a willow in her hand   10
  Upon the wild sea banks, and waft her love
  To come again to Carthage.

JESSICA

                In such a night
  Medea gathered the enchanted herbs
  That did renew old Æson.

LORENZO

                In such a night
  Did Jessica steal from the wealthy Jew,   15

16 *unthrift*   one who spends money carelessly.

11 *vows*   promises.

21 *shrew*   a woman who nags.

22 *Slander*   tell untrue tales about.

23 *out-night you*   Jessica is referring to the opening lines 'In such a night'. She says that she could keep the game going longer than Lorenzo could.

30 *stray*   wander.

And with an unthrift love did run from Venice
As far as Belmont.

JESSICA

           In such a night
Did young Lorenzo swear he loved her well,
Stealing her soul with many vows of faith,
And ne'er a true one.

LORENZO

                In such a night   20
Did pretty Jessica, like a little shrew,
Slander her love, and he forgave it her.

JESSICA

I would out-night you did nobody come:
But hark, I hear the footing of a man.

Enter STEPHANO.

LORENZO

Who comes so fast in silence of the night?   25

STEPHANO

A friend!

LORENZO

A friend! what friend? your name, I pray you,
    friend?

STEPHANO

Stephano is my name, and I bring word
My mistress will before the break of day
Be here at Belmont. She doth stray about   30
By holy crosses, where she kneels and prays
For happy wedlock hours.

LORENZO

                Who comes with her?

33 *hermit* holy man who lives by himself, avoiding contact with the world. When Portia left Belmont she said that she was going to a monastery for a while.

39 *Sola! . . . sola!* Launcelot is trying to sound like the horn the messenger would have blown on his arrival.

43 *hollowing* shouting.

46 *a post* messenger.

47 *horn full of good news* Launcelot could be referring to the messenger's horn, saying that it signals the bringing of good news, or else he might be picturing the messenger's postbag as a 'horn of plenty' – literally full of good news.

49 *expect* await.

STEPHANO

None but a holy hermit and her maid.
I pray you, is my master yet returned?

LORENZO

He is not, nor we have not heard from him. –   35
But go we in, I pray thee, Jessica,
And ceremoniously let us prepare
Some welcome for the mistress of the house.

Enter LAUNCELOT.

LAUNCELOT

Sola, sola, wo ha, ho! sola, sola!

LORENZO

Who calls?   40

LAUNCELOT

Sola! did you see Master Lorenzo? Master Lorenzo,
sola, sola!

LORENZO

Leave hollowing man; here!

LAUNCELOT

Sola! where, where?

LORENZO

Here!   45

LAUNCELOT

Tell him there's a post come from my master, with
his horn full of good news; my master will be here
ere morning.

Exit

LORENZO

Sweet soul, let's in, and there expect their coming.

51–2 *signify . . . house*   let those inside the house hear this news.

57 *Become . . . harmony*   are suitable for the sounds of sweet music.

59 *patens*   small dishes like those used in Communion services. Lorenzo imagines that they see the 'floor of heaven' from beneath and that the stars are really golden dishes.

60 *orb*   star.

61 *But in . . . sings*   it was believed that the stars moved on a fixed circuit (or 'sphere'). As they moved they each made a beautiful sound. All the stars together produced 'the music of the spheres'.

62 *quiring*   singing (as in a choir).

cherubin   one of the many types of angels in Heaven.

64–5 *Whilst this muddy vesture . . . hear it*   whilst we are trapped in our bodies, i.e. still living, we cannot hear this heavenly music.

66 *Diana*   goddess of the moon.

67 *touches*   touches on the musical instruments.

70 *spirits are*   mind is.

71 *wanton*   thoughtless.

72 *unhandled colts*   young horses which have not been broken-in (trained).

73 *Fetching mad bounds*   leaping madly about.

74 *hot condition of their blood*   they are naturally excitable.

And yet no matter; why should we go in?   50
My friend Stephano, signify, I pray you,
Within the house, your mistress is at hand,
And bring your music forth into the air.

Exit STEPHANO

How sweet the moonlight sleeps upon this bank!
Here will we sit, and let the sounds of music   55
Creep in our ears; soft stillness and the night
Become the touches of sweet harmony.
Sit, Jessica. Look how the floor of heaven
Is thick inlaid with patens of bright gold;
There's not the smallest orb which thou behold'st 60
But in his motion like an angel sings,
Still quiring to the young-eyed cherubins;
Such harmony is in immortal souls,
But whilst this muddy vesture of decay
Doth grossly close it in, we cannot hear it.   65

Enter MUSICIANS.

Come, ho! and wake Diana with a hymn!
With sweetest touches pierce your mistress' ear,
And draw her home with music.

Music

JESSICA
    I am never merry when I hear sweet music.

LORENZO
    The reason is your spirits are attentive;   70
    For do but note a wild and wanton herd
    Or race of youthful and unhandled colts
    Fetching mad bounds, bellowing and neighing loud,
    Which is the hot condition of their blood.

75 *perchance*   by chance.

77 *Make a mutual stand*   they all stand still together.

80 *Did feign*   did make up.

  Orpheus   legendary Greek poet and musician who had the gift of charming even inanimate objects with his music.

81 *naught so stockish*   nothing that is so insensitive.

84 *concord*   peaceful harmony.

85 *stratagems*   plans (usually of a military nature).

  spoils   the general destruction or looting that happens after battle.

86 *motions of his spirit*   his sensitivity.

87 *Erebus*   the dark country under the earth that the dead have to go through before they reach the Underworld (Hades).

88 *Mark*   pay attention to.

91 *naughty*   evil.

95–7 *his state . . . waters*   the imposter's supposed glory is as totally overwhelmed by the real king's glory as the waters of a stream are swallowed up by the sea.

If they but hear perchance a trumpet sound,　　75
Or any air of music touch their ears,
You shall perceive them make a mutual stand,
Their savage eyes turned to a modest gaze
By the sweet power of music. Therefore the poet
Did feign that Orpheus drew trees, stones, and
　　floods,　　80
Since naught so stockish, hard, and full of rage,
But music for the time doth change his nature.
The man that hath no music in himself,
Nor is not moved with concord of sweet sounds,
Is fit for treasons, stratagems, and spoils;　　85
The motions of his spirit are dull as night,
And his affections dark as Erebus;
Let no such man be trusted. – Mark the music.

Enter PORTIA *and* NERISSA, *at a distance from the others.*

PORTIA

That light we see is burning in my hall.
How far that little candle throws his beams!　　90
So shines a good deed in a naughty world.

NERISSA

When the moon shone, we did not see the candle.

PORTIA

So doth the greater glory dim the less;
A substitute shines brightly as a king
Until a king be by, and then his state　　95
Empties itself, as doth an inland brook
Into the main of waters. – Music! hark!

NERISSA

It is your music, madam, of the house.

99   *without respect*   unless it is contrasted with something else.

101   *bestows*   gives it (the virtue of sounding sweeter).

103   *attended*   listened to, or perhaps, heard together.

107–8   *How many things . . . perfection!*   how many things are appreciated fully because they appear at the right time.

109   *Endymion*   in Greek legend Endymion was a beautiful young man who was loved by the moon goddess. In order to preserve both his youth and beauty she cast a spell of eternal sleep over him.

115   *Which speed . . . our words*   we hope that our husbands are doing well as a result of our prayers.

PORTIA

Nothing is good, I see, without respect;
Methinks it sounds much sweeter than by day.   100

NERISSA

Silence bestows that virtue on it, madam.

PORTIA

The crow doth sing as sweetly as the lark
When neither is attended; and I think
The nightingale, if she should sing by day,
When every goose is cackling, would be thought   105
No better a musician than the wren!
How many things by season seasoned are
To their right praise, and true perfection!
Peace! – how the moon sleeps with Endymion,
And would not be awaked!

Music ceases.

LORENZO

                    That is the voice,   110
Or I am much deceived, of Portia.

PORTIA

He knows me as the blind man knows the cuckoo –
By the bad voice!

LORENZO

          Dear lady, welcome home!

PORTIA

We have been praying for our husbands' welfare,
Which speed, we hope, the better for our words.   115
Are they returned?

LORENZO

          Madam, they are not yet;

118 *signify*   indicate.

119–20 *they take No note*   they do not take any notice, they do not mention.

120 *hence*   from here.

127–8 *we should hold . . . sun*   the Antipodes are the lands on the other side of the earth. Bassanio is suggesting that Portia lightens their darkness to such a degree that they have no need of the sun.

129 *be light*   immoral, unfaithful.

130 *heavy husband*   unhappy husband.

132 *God sort all!*   let God sort it all out.

135 *bound*   indebted.

But there is come a messenger before
To signify their coming.

PORTIA

Go in, Nerissa.
Give order to my servants that they take
No note at all of our being absent hence;   120
Nor you, Lorenzo; Jessica, nor you.

A tucket sounds.

LORENZO

Your husband is at hand; I hear his trumpet;
We are no tell-tales, madam; fear you not.

PORTIA

This night methinks is but the daylight sick;
It looks a little paler – 't is a day   125
Such as the day is when the sun is hid.

Enter BASSANIO, ANTONIO, GRATIANO, *and their followers.*

BASSANIO

We should hold day with the Antipodes,
If you would walk in absence of the sun.

PORTIA

Let me *give* light, but let me not *be* light,
For a light wife doth make a heavy husband,   130
And never be Bassanio so for me. –
But God sort all! You are welcome home, my
    lord.

BASSANIO

I thank you, madam. Give welcome to my friend;
This is the man, this is Antonio,
To whom I am so infinitely bound.   135

138 *aquitted of* Antonio is saying that all debts have now been cleared; both his debt to Shylock, and Bassanio's debt to him.

140–1 *It must appear . . . courtesy* your welcome will be apparent through more than just words, therefore I am not going to spend long on polite words.

144 *gelt* gelded, castrated.

147 *paltry* worthless.

148–50 *whose posy was . . . knife* the verse engraved by the knife-maker on a knife he makes.

155 *vehement oaths* strong vows.

156 *You should have been respective* you should have respected (your vehement oaths).

PORTIA

You should in all sense be much bound to him,
For, as I hear, he was much bound for you.

ANTONIO

No more than I am well acquitted of.

PORTIA

(*To* ANTONIO) Sir, you are very welcome to our
house.
It must appear in other ways than words;   140
Therefore I scant this breathing courtesy.

GRATIANO

(*To* NERISSA) By yonder moon I swear you do me
wrong;
In faith I gave it to the judge's clerk
Would he were gelt that had it for my part,
Since you do take it, love, so much at heart.   145

PORTIA

A quarrel, ho, already! What's the matter?

GRATIANO

About a hoop of gold, a paltry ring
That she did give me, whose posy was
For all the world like cutler's poetry
Upon a knife: "Love me, and leave me not."   150

NERISSA

What talk you of the posy or the value?
You swore to me when I did give it you
That you would wear it till your hour of death,
And that it should lie with you in your grave.
Though not for me, yet for your vehement oaths   155
You should have been respective and have kept it.

158 *The clerk . . . had it* the clerk who had the ring will never grow to be a man and wear a beard.

162 *scrubbèd* short.

164 *prating* to prate is to talk at great length about nothing important.

169 *riveted* fastened firmly.

172 *I dare be sworn for him* I am willing to swear, on his behalf.

174 *masters* contains.

176 *An't were to me* if it were me, if I were in Nerissa's place. Portia knows that she is in the same position, and traps Bassanio into admitting as much.

Gave it a judge's clerk! no, God's my judge,
The clerk will ne'er wear hair on's face that had it.

GRATIANO

He will, and if he live to be a man.

NERISSA

Ay, if a woman live to be a man.   160

GRATIANO

Now, by this hand, I gave it to a youth,
A kind of boy, a little scrubbèd boy,
No higher than thyself, the judge's clerk,
A prating boy that begged it as a fee.
I could not for my heart deny it him.   165

PORTIA

You were to blame, I must be plain with you,
To part so slightly with your wife's first gift,
A thing stuck on with oaths upon your finger,
And so riveted with faith unto your flesh.
I gave my love a ring, and made him swear   170
Never to part with it, and here he stands:
I dare be sworn for him he would not leave it,
Nor pluck it from his finger, for the wealth
That the world masters. Now, in faith, Gratiano,
You give your wife too unkind a cause of grief;   175
An 't were to me I should be mad at it.

BASSANIO (Aside)

Why, I were best to cut my left hand off,
And swear I lost the ring defending it.

GRATIANO

My Lord Bassanio gave his ring away
Unto the judge that begged it, and indeed   180
Deserved it too; and then the boy, his clerk,

183   *aught* anything.

189   *Even so . . . truth* your lying heart is as empty of the truth as your finger is bar of the ring.

198   *abate . . . displeasure* you would not be so angry.

200   *worthiness* worth.

201   *contain* keep.

203–6   *What man . . . ceremony* surely no man could be so unreasonable or so uncaring as to demand the symbol of our love, if only you had defended it (the ring) with any degree of sincerity.

That took some pains in writing, he begged mine,
And neither man nor master would take aught
But the two rings.

PORTIA

What ring gave you, my lord?
Not that, I hope, which you received of me.   185

BASSANIO

If I could add a lie unto a fault,
I would deny it; but you see my finger
Hath not the ring upon it; it is gone.

PORTIA

Even so void is your false heart of truth.
By heaven I will ne'er come in your bed   190
Until I see the ring!

NERISSA

(*To* GRATIANO)   Nor I in yours
Till I again see mine!

BASSANIO

Sweet Portia,
If you did know to whom I gave the ring,
If you did know for whom I gave the ring,
And would conceive for what I gave the ring,   195
And how unwillingly I left the ring,
When nought would be accepted but the ring,
You would abate the strength of your displeasure.

PORTIA

If you had known the virtue of the ring,
Or half her worthiness that gave the ring,   200
Or your own honour to contain the ring,
You would not then have parted with the ring.
What man is there so much unreasonable,

210 *civil doctor* a doctor of the kind of law that deals specifically with the rights of citizens.

214 *held up the very life* upheld, defended the life.

216 *enforced* compelled.

217 *beset* overcome.

courtesy good manners.

219 *besmear it* spoil it.

220 *blessèd candles* the stars.

226 *as liberal* generous to a fault, both with possessions and the body.

229 *Know him* the verb 'to know' can also mean 'to have sex with'. It is used in this way in the Bible and Shakespeare's audience would have appreciated the pun.

230 *Lie not a night* do not sleep away from home, not even for a night.

Argus a watchman with a hundred eyes, employed by Hera, Queen of the Greek gods.

233 *I'll have . . . bedfellow* I'll sleep with this civil doctor. Portia's statement sounds shocking. In fact, she tells the truth; if Bassanio is away overnight she will sleep with herself. This is another example of dramatic irony.

If you had pleased to have defended it
With any terms of zeal, wanted the modesty   205
To urge the thing held as a ceremony?
Nerissa teaches me what to believe:
I'll die for 't, but some woman had the ring!

BASSANIO

No, by my honour, madam, by my soul,
No woman had it, but a civil doctor,   210
Which did refuse three thousand ducats of me,
And begged the ring; the which I did deny him,
And suffered him to go displeased away,
Even he that had held up the very life
Of my dear friend. What should I say, sweet lady? 215
I was enforced to send it after him;
I was beset with shame and courtesy;
My honour would not let ingratitude
So much besmear it. Pardon me, good lady,
For by these blessèd candles of the night,   220
Had you been there, I think you would have
    begged
The ring of me to give the worthy doctor.

PORTIA

Let not that doctor e'er come near my house.
Since he hath got the jewel that I loved,
And that which you did swear to keep for me,   225
I will become as liberal as you;
I'll not deny him anything I have,
No, not my body, nor my husband's bed;
Know him I shall, I am well sure of it.
Lie not a night from home. Watch me like Argus; 230
If you do not, if I be left alone,
Now by mine honour, which is yet mine own,
I'll have that doctor for my bedfellow.

234–5 *be well advised . . . protection*   think carefully when you leave me to my own devices.

236 *take him*   catch him.

237 *mar*   spoil.

pen   the pen the clerk writes with, but 'pen' in this context also means penis.

240 *enforcèd wrong*   this wrong thing I was compelled to do.

243 *Mark you but that*   note that.

245 *double self*   the double reflection, but also a reference to the fact that Bassanio i 'two-faced' or devious.

246 *an oath of credit*   a worthwhile promise.

251 *quite miscarried*   the plan would have gone completely wrong.

NERISSA

And I his clerk; therefore be well advised
How you do leave me to mine own protection.　　235

GRATIANO

Well, do you so; let not me take him then,
For if I do, I'll mar the young clerk's pen.

ANTONIO

I am th' unhappy subject of these quarrels.

PORTIA

Sir, grieve not you; you are welcome notwithstand-
　　ing.

BASSANIO

Portia, forgive me this enforcèd wrong,　　240
And, in the hearing of these many friends,
I swear to thee, even by thine own fair eyes,
Wherein I see myself –

PORTIA

　　　　　　　　　Mark you but that
In both my eyes he doubly sees himself;
In each eye one; swear by your double self,　　245
And there's an oath of credit.

BASSANIO

　　　　　　　　　Nay, but hear me.
Pardon this fault, and by my soul I swear
I never more will break an oath with thee.

ANTONIO

I once did lend my body for his wealth
Which, but for him that had your husband's
　　ring,　　250
Had quite miscarried. I dare be bound again,

253   *advisedly*   if he thinks about it.

254   *surety*   guarantor, someone who backs up a loan if the borrower fails to pay it back.

262   *in lieu of this*   for this.

264   *ways . . . enough!*   the roads are in good condition, i.e. do not need repairing. Gratiano is saying that there was no need for he and Bassanio to apologise when their wives have apparently broken their vows also.

265   *cuckolds*   husbands whose wives have been unfaithful to them, in much the same way as the cuckoo lays her eggs in other birds' nests.

266   *grossly*   rudely.

271   *Shall witness*   will confirm.

272   *even but now*   only recently.

My soul upon the forfeit, that your lord
Will never more break faith advisedly.

PORTIA

Then you shall be his surety. Give him this,
And bid him keep it better than the other.   255

She gives ANTONIO *a ring.*

ANTONIO

Here, Lord Bassanio, swear to keep this ring.

BASSANIO

By heaven it is the same I gave the doctor!

PORTIA

I had it of him; pardon me, Bassanio,
For by this ring the doctor lay with me.

NERISSA

And pardon me, my gentle Gratiano,   260
For that same scrubbèd boy, the doctor's clerk,
In lieu of this, last night did lie with me.

GRATIANO

Why this is like the mending of highways
In summer, where the ways are fair enough!
What, are we cuckolds ere we have deserved it?   265

PORTIA

Speak not so grossly. You are all amazed;
Here is a letter; read it at your leisure;
It comes from Padua, from Bellario.
There you shall find that Portia was the doctor,
Nerissa there her clerk. Lorenzo here   270
Shall witness I set forth as soon as you,
And even but now returned; I have not yet
Entered my house. Antonio, you are welcome,

277   *suddenly*   i.e. their return was not expected.

279   *chancèd on*   came upon.

 dumb   speechless, lost for words.

282–3   *but the clerk . . . man*   Nerissa says that she will never be unfaithful to Gratiano unless the impossible happens and she becomes a man.

284–5   *you shall be . . .my wife*   see note to Act 5, scene 1, line 233.

288   *safely come to road*   safely anchored in the harbour.

And I have better news in store for you
Than you expect. Unseal this letter soon;   275
There you shall find three of your argosies
Are richly come to harbour suddenly.
You shall not know by what strange accident
I chancèd on this letter.

ANTONIO

I am dumb!

BASSANIO

Were you the doctor, and I knew you not?   280

GRATIANO

Were you the clerk that is to make me cuckold?

NERISSA

Ay, but the clerk that never means to do it,
Unless he live until he be a man.

BASSANIO

Sweet doctor, you shall be my bedfellow;
When I am absent then lie with my wife.   285

ANTONIO

Sweet lady, you have given me life and living;
For here I read for certain that my ships
Are safely come to road.

PORTIA

                    How now, Lorenzo?
My clerk hath some good comforts too for you.

NERISSA

Ay, and I'll give them him without a fee.   290
There do I give to you and Jessica,
From the rich Jew, a special deed of gift,
After his death, of all he dies possessed of.

249

294 *manna* food given to the Israelites by God to keep them from starving on their long journey through the desert. It miraculously appeared every morning. Used here it means that Lorenzo can hardly believe the good news that Portia has given him. He and Jessica need the money that Shylock will provide.

296–7 *not satisfied . . . full* you have not learnt everything that you would like to know about these events.

298 *charge us* we will answer as if we were under oath in court.

inter'gatories questions.

302 *rather stay* rather wait (to go to bed).

305 *couching* sharing the same bed.

307 *So sore* so much.

LORENZO

Fair ladies, you drop manna in the way
Of starvèd people.

PORTIA

              It is almost morning,   295
And yet I am sure you are not satisfied
Of these events at full. Let us go in,
And charge us there upon inter'gatories,
And we will answer all things faithfully.

GRATIANO

Let it be so; the first inter'gatory   300
That my Nerissa shall be sworn on is,
Whether till the next night she had rather stay,
Or go to bed now, being two hours to day;
But were the day come, I should wish it dark
Till I were couching with the doctor's clerk.   305
Well, while I live I'll fear no other thing
So sore as keeping safe Nerissa's ring.

Exeunt

Study programme

Before reading the play

Language

If you have already read the section on Shakespeare's language in the 'Introduction' (page xiii) you will know that you can expect to encounter many different kinds of speeches in the play. Some will be written in poetry, and some will be written in prose. Some will be angry, some romantic, and some will be funny. It all depends on the character who is talking and the role of that character in the play.

1 Read through the following extracts:

- describe the type of speech each one is;
- say something about the kind of characters who are talking.

LORENZO

    The moon shines bright. In such a night as this,
    When the sweet wind did gently kiss the trees,
    And they did make no noise, in such a night
    Troilus methinks mounted the Trojan walls,
    And sighed his soul towards the Grecian tents
    Where Cressid lay that night.

                                      (Act 5, scene 1, lines 1–6)

SHYLOCK

    I'll have my bond. I will not hear thee speak;
    I'll have my bond, and therefore speak no more.
    I'll not be made a soft and dull-eyed fool,
    To shake the head, relent, and sigh, and yield
    To Christian intercessors. (*He turns to go*) Follow not –
    I'll have no speaking; I will have my bond.

                                    (Act 3, scene 3, lines 12–17)

PORTIA

> The quality of mercy is not strained;
> It droppeth as the gentle rain from heaven
> Upon the place beneath; it is twice blest:
> It blesseth him that gives, and him that takes;
> 'T is mightiest in the mightiest; it becomes
> The thronèd monarch better than his crown.

(Act 4, scene 1, lines 180–5)

Characters

1. It is always a good idea to gather information about the major characters as you read through a play, and an even better idea to make a note of key speeches that give you important insights into these characters. Once a major character has been introduced you should ask yourself exactly what information we have been given about him/her. Try to decide what your own reaction to this character is. Do you like the person? Why? Why not?

Having made a note of your first impression of this character, stop at various stages throughout the play to see if your opinion has changed at all. If it has, try to pinpoint exactly why this change has taken place.

2. So much for the major characters, but we must not forget the supporting cast of minor characters. Just how important are they?

One way to answer this question is to look at where the minor characters appear in the play and how Shakespeare uses them. Minor characters can:

- be present in order to give the audience information. Look at the beginning of Act 3. What are we being told here?
- exist so that the major characters have someone to confide in. In this way the audience can find out what the major characters are thinking and feeling. It is for precisely this reason that a lot of television heroes have a 'sidekick', someone they can explain things to. As you read the play look out for Portia's 'sidekick'. What kinds of things do we find out when Portia talks to her?
- exist to provide a touch of light relief. You should be able to spot the

254

clown of the play quite easily, but think carefully about the role Gratiano plays. He may be one of Bassanio's best friends, but is that his only function in the play?

As you go through the play making your character notes, do not forget to add a line or two about the minor characters. They are more important than they first appear to be.

Plot

▓ As in most of Shakespeare's plays there are really several stories that run side by side throughout *The Merchant of Venice*. In order to help you sort out the different stories read the act summaries (at the beginning of each act) and write brief notes about the events surrounding three of the men in the play: Antonio, Bassanio and Lorenzo. The notes for each man must only contain an account of the events that that particular character takes part in.

▓ Having identified the different stories that *The Merchant of Venice* contains you need to be able to place them in order of importance and make some observations about the way in which they are used. The central story is called the plot, the second story is the sub-plot and the least important story is a secondary sub-plot (or a sub-sub-plot!). Draw a flow chart for each of the three plots. The flow charts should be headed *Plot*, *Sub-plot* and *Sub-sub-plot*. You should be able to put in some details from the act summaries but later, as you read through the play, you will be able to look at each scene individually and decide which plot each one contains details of. Enter the details, with the act and scene number, on the appropriate flow chart. Do this until you have finished the play.

▓ As your charts begin to grow you should notice some interesting patterns. Sometimes characters move from one plot to carry out an action in another plot. Colour code your characters and draw in arrows to show exactly where this happens.

Using a different colour, trace the development of the play scene by scene, moving between the plot lines as necessary. What kind of pattern can you see in the way in which Shakespeare moves from plot to plot?

Shakespeare may never have intended *The Merchant of Venice* to be 'taken apart' in quite this fashion, but there is a lot you can learn from keeping such a record, and all of it will be useful when you come to look at the activities in the 'After reading' section (page 264).

Themes

When people talk about the theme of a play they are really talking about the important ideas that the play is built around. Justice, the power of love and money, the desire for revenge, and the existence of different kinds of prejudice are all important themes in *The Merchant of Venice*. In order to discover exactly where these themes appear in the play you need to look very carefully at what the main characters say and do.

1 Keep a record of important lines in the play by drawing spider diagrams. The centre of each diagram should contain a theme and the outer circles should contain quotations relevant to that particular theme.

2 Repeat the spider diagram exercise, this time using it to make a note of which scenes the themes appear in. Studying the two sets of diagrams will give you an indication of what the most important themes are. (Look for the diagrams that have the largest number of outer circles.)

3 Make a note of the images that occur in connection with the various themes. When you have finished the play look back at your notes and see if certain images are used for each theme. You may not find the same image being used very often but any examples of repetition are worth noting. When you have decided which images accompany each theme record your findings on a chart, either by providing a written description of the images or by drawing them.

Drama

Before you begin the play try the following class improvisations.

▓ Imagine that you are already heavily indebted to a friend, who may have lent you money or done you a favour that has put them to considerable trouble; they may even have saved your life. You now find yourself in a situation where you must go back and ask for yet more help. How will you approach your friend? Will you be honest, embarrassed, angry about having to ask? Will you resort to flattery in an attempt to get what you want? How are you prepared to cope with rejection?

▓ Now imagine that you must ask your worst enemy for help. Again think about how you would approach someone you loath and despise in order to ask for something.

▓ Choose one of the improvisations and turn it into a story. Try to describe the thoughts and feelings of your characters as carefully as you can so that the difficulties of either situation can be fully appreciated by your readers.

During reading

Act 1

Check your knowledge of Act 1

- Money will be an important factor in the play. What do we learn about the money that Antonio, Bassanio and Portia possess? Locate and make a note of the lines that give you this information.
- What reasons do Salerio and Solanio suggest to account for Antonio's sadness?
- How has Bassanio managed to spend all his money?
- Whose idea was the test of the caskets, and why does Portia feel that she has to abide by this restriction?
- Describe the suitors that Portia has received so far. What is her opinion of each of them?
- Find the lines that suggest that Bassanio will be welcomed if he arrives to woo Portia.

- What do we learn about Shylock in this act? Include as many details as possible about the life he leads and the kind of person he appears to be.
- What reasons does Shylock give for hating Antonio?
- What are the exact terms of the bargain that Antonio agrees to?

Questioning the text in Act 1

1 How would you describe the relationship between Antonio and Bassanio? Using any information provided by this first act, write an imaginative account that reconstructs their relationship in the years preceding the play.

2 Why do Salerio and Solanio appear in this act? In your opinion is this an effective way of presenting background information?

3 Using the impression created by Gratiano's behaviour and your own imagination, write a detailed physical description of this character, paying careful attention to the way in which he might have dressed. Does there appear to be any value in what he says or is it all complete nonsense?

4 Look carefully at Bassanio's first description of Portia. What does this description stress? Do you find this emphasis either odd or distasteful? Explain your reaction.

5 Jason and the Golden Fleece will be referred to again later in the play. Research the story and write your own account of the main events. In what way is Bassanio like Jason?

6 Reread the descriptions of Portia's suitors. Using the glossary notes to help you, explain exactly how you think an Elizabethan audience might have reacted to each description.

7 What do we learn about the relationship between the Christian and the Jewish communities in Venice at this time? Suggest a number of practical reasons that would have made it difficult for people from the two faiths to interact socially.

▣ Try to find out something about the position of moneylenders in Elizabethan England. Why do the Jews in the play make money in this way and
not the Christians?

▣ Look carefully at the use of prose and blank verse in this act. What is
gained by writing speeches in verse, and why do you think Shakespeare
chooses to limit his use of this style?

Act 2

Check your knowledge of Act 2

- What do we learn about the Prince of Morocco in this act?
- What reasons does Launcelot give for wanting to leave Shylock to go and
work for Bassanio?
- What has life in Shylock's house been like for Jessica? Look carefully at
both what she says and Shylock's instructions to her before he leaves to
go to supper.
- What reason does Shylock give for not wanting to go and have supper with
Bassanio? Why does he finally make up his mind to go?
- Describe Jessica's escape from Shylock's house.
- Explain Morocco's reasons for choosing the gold casket. What is he told
by the scroll inside the casket?
- How do we know that Lorenzo and Jessica do not go to Belmont with
Bassanio?
- What hints are there in this act that Antonio may have difficulty in paying
back his loan?
- What reasons does the Prince of Arragon give for choosing the silver
casket? What does the scroll tell him?

Questioning the text in Act 2

▣ Launcelot Gobbo provides most of the comedy in the play. With the
passage of time, however, much of what he says has become obscure. Can

you suggest any ways of staging his first scene so that it remains humorous? (There are some clues in the text.)

2 In what way is Gratiano different from the character we met in Act 1? Can you suggest a reason for this?

3 Imagine that you are telling a friend about Jessica. Describe her in as much detail as possible (we learn a lot about her character in this act), and say how you think she feels about her father.

4 Look carefully at Gratiano's speech in Act 2, scene 6, lines 8–19. Compare this with what Salerio, Solanio and Shylock have already said about ships in Act 1. What is being stressed in all these references? Why do you think this is?

5 Using the glossary notes to help you, explain the word play between Jessica and Lorenzo in scene 6. Why might some of the humour be lost in a modern production?

6 Reread Salerio's description of the parting of Antonio and Bassanio, then write a short scene that covers this event. You must use the information that Salerio provides – the rest can be pure invention.

7 Compare the characters of Bassanio and Lorenzo. In what ways are they similar and in what ways different? Does Bassanio appear to have altered in his attitude towards Portia since Act 1?

8 Using the plot charts you produced (page 255), explain how dramatic tension is built up in this act. Why is so much of this act devoted to the secondary sub-plot? What effect does this create?

Act 3

Check your knowledge of Act 3

• What reasons does Shylock give in this act for wanting to take his revenge on Antonio? What does he mention here that he did not mention in Act 1?

- Find the lines that suggest that Shylock is more upset about his missing gold than the disappearance of his daughter.

- Explain why Portia is reluctant to let Bassanio take the test of the caskets.

- What are Bassanio's reasons for choosing the lead casket?

- What condition did Gratiano have to agree to when he asked Nerissa to marry him?

- Why do Lorenzo and Jessica arrive at Portia's house?

- What reason does Antonio give for Shylock wanting to take his life?

- What does Portia tell Lorenzo she will do until Bassanio's return?

- Why does Launcelot tell Jessica that she is damned? Give both reasons. How does Jessica believe she will be saved?

Questioning the text in Act 3

1. What is different about the presentation of Shylock in the first scene? At what point do you feel the most sympathy for him? Where does he start to lose our sympathy again?

2. How has the elopement of Jessica added to Shylock's hatred of Antonio? Do you find this unreasonable?

3. Bassanio's speech before he chooses the caskets contains several images designed to prove that things should not be judged by their outward appearance. Take at least two of these images and explain them in detail. Do they appear to have any connection with other images used in the play?

4. What do we learn has been happening in Venice from Salerio's speech in Act 3, scene 2, lines 270–282? Write a short scene that shows the Duke attempting to persuade Shylock to abandon his case against Antonio.

5. Imagine that Bassanio writes a reply to Antonio telling him that he is on his way to Venice with money to pay back the loan. How will Bassanio try to raise Antonio's spirits? Write the letter.

6⃣ Look carefully at Shylock's speeches in scene 3. Explain how the way in which they have been written emphasises Shylock's determination.

7⃣ What reason does Portia give for wanting to help Antonio? Do you find this reaction unusual? How else might she have reacted?

8⃣ How does Portia's anticipation of her disguise differ from Jessica's reaction in similar circumstances? Why do you think this is?

9⃣ Looking back over the three casket scenes what is the overall message conveyed by this story? Does this message have any relevance to the main plot?

Act 4

Check your knowledge of Act 4

- Find the lines in both this act and Act 3 that tell us that the Duke is on Antonio's side.
- What does Shylock suggest will happen if he does not receive justice?
- How does Antonio react to the fact that his life is in danger?
- How does Portia first try to persuade Shylock to abandon his claim?
- What two conditions prevent Shylock from taking his pound of flesh?
- Why are Shylock's goods confiscated and his own life threatened?
- What is the final outcome of the trial? Describe all the conditions imposed on Shylock.
- What does Bassanio initially offer Portia as payment for her part in the trial?
- Why is Bassanio so reluctant to let her have the ring? Why does he change his mind?

Questioning the text in Act 4

1⃣ Describe the attitude of the main characters towards Shylock. Which of these attitudes can you identify most closely with?

2. What more do we learn about Antonio's state of mind in this scene? Is this consistent with his actions in the play? Can you offer any explanation for his attitude?

3. What does this scene tell us about Portia? Is anything she does here, from making her great speech about mercy through to her refusal to show Shylock any mercy, a total surprise in the light of what we have already seen of her? Show how her earlier appearances prepare us for her performance in court.

4. Bearing in mind Shylock's religious beliefs, explain why Portia's mercy speech fails to move him. Write an alternative speech that does not rely so heavily on Christian teaching.

5. Draw a graph that charts the emotional peaks of the court scene. What do these 'high points' have in common?

6. Can you suggest any reasons for not finishing this act with the exit of Shylock? Do you approve or disapprove of the way in which the scene finishes?

7. Why do you think that the encounter between Gratiano and Portia was made a separate scene? How does it form a 'bridge' between Act 4 and Act 5?

Act 5

Check your knowledge of Act 5

- What kinds of people are Jessica and Lorenzo talking about at the beginning of this act? What do all three examples have in common?
- How is the argument about the rings first introduced?
- Who does Portia say must have been given the rings?
- What part does Antonio play in restoring the peace between husband and wife?

Questioning the text in Act 5

1 Why do you think Shakespeare chose to end the play in Belmont rather than Venice? What do we gain from this extra scene? Explain how themes that have been introduced earlier are now finally resolved.

2 Discuss the difference in mood between Act 4 and the beginning of Act 5. What dramatic purpose does this contrast serve?

3 What do the rings symbolise? Do you think that Portia was right to care so much about them? What has Bassanio learnt from this experience?

4 Explain how you would group the characters at various points in this act in order to emphasise the antagonism and reconciliation that we witness. One character must remain alone. Why is this? How else are we made aware of his isolation?

After reading

Plot

For some of these activities it will help if you have the plot charts you produced (page 255) close at hand.

1 You have been given the task of staging a production of *The Merchant of Venice*. The producers who have employed you have made it clear that, in their opinion, the play is too long. They have therefore instructed you to remove several scenes in order to reduce the running time of the play.

   a) Look carefully at your plot charts and decide which scenes you think could be removed. When you have done this, prepare a report for the producers listing the scenes you intend to remove, giving reasons for your choice. Remember to consider what the effect of removing these scenes will be on the play as a whole.

   b) As a director and a lover of Shakespeare's work you are horrified by the report. Write a letter to the producers explaining why the play should not be cut. Your letter will be much more effective if you use examples from the text to show what will be lost, rather than just making vague generalisations.

2️⃣ Work in groups for this task.

a) Look at your plot charts again. Are there any patterns that you can see in the way in which Shakespeare uses the stories? Try to work out some reasons for any patterns that you come across.

b) You are now going to try to rearrange the play! Obviously you cannot reverse the storylines, but that is the only restriction that you face. You may remove some scenes altogether if you wish to do so.

Discuss how the scenes could be rearranged. Try to work out at least two possible ways of restructuring the play, and then choose which of these ideas you like best. Make a list of reasons for using your version of the play rather than the original.

c) Now present both your new play, and your arguments for your reshaping of it to other people.

Once you have finished your work you can either appoint a group spokesperson to report back to the class, or else each member of the group can prepare their own report on the work that has taken place. Make sure that you explain yourself clearly when you do this. If, for example, you have decided to start the play in Belmont rather than Venice, your audience must know why you have made this decision.

3️⃣ The sub-plot owes more than a little to traditional fairy tales. The following tasks are designed to help you appreciate how Shakespeare could take such a story and yet use it in a realistic way, so that the characters are no longer a beautiful princess and a handsome prince, but become real people.

a) Make a list of everything in the sub-plot that could easily appear in a fairy tale. You have been given one clue.

b) When you have finished your list, use it to write the story of 'Portia and the Three Caskets'. This story should be as close to a proper fairy tale as you can make it. If it helps, imagine that it is to be read to a group of five- and six-year-old children.

c) Now go back to the play and look at the scenes that contain the sub-plot. Compare Shakespeare's version of the story with your own. How has he gone beyond the basic story and made his characters come alive?

d) When you have completed all the tasks listed here answer one of the following essay questions: 'At first sight the sub-plot of *The Merchant of Venice* would appear to be nothing more than a fairy tale designed to provide a contrast to the main action of the play. A closer look at Shakespeare's treatment of the story, however, soon reveals just how far beyond the traditional trappings of the story he has gone.' Discuss.

OR

To what extent would you agree with the statement that, 'the sub-plot of *The Merchant of Venice* is just another fairy tale'?

4 Venice and Belmont are, in many ways, the opposite of each other. Venice is a commercial city. We hear its citizens talk of trading vessels and shipwrecks, and we see them drawing up complicated legal papers to finalise a business deal. Belmont, on the other hand, is where we meet a beautiful woman wooed by a Moorish prince, and where we see two lovers listening to romantic music in a moonlit garden.

Put together a display that shows the differences between the two places. The most effective way of presenting such a display is to create a collage of pictures and words, each depicting some aspect of either Venice or Belmont. These pictures and words can be drawn directly onto your display paper, or produced separately and then mounted on a display board.

To make the differences between the two places even clearer, divide your display in two so that you can use half your space to represent Venice, and half to represent Belmont.

5 The action of the play covers several months and yet some scenes take place within hours of each other. Produce two time lines (one for Venice and one for Belmont) showing when the events of the various plots occur in relation to one another.

6 Imagine that Portia's strategy did not succeed and that Shylock won his case and killed Antonio. Write an outline for an alternative ending to the play. You will need to consider the effect of such an outcome on Bassanio and Portia (and by extension, Gratiano and Nerissa), Jessica and Lorenzo, and Shylock himself.

Characters

1 a) Make a note of what each character says about him or herself. Indicate which statements you agree with and which you disagree with. If you disagree with any statement you must give your reasons.

b) Try to put together a profile of each of the main characters using only their own words. Which characters say the most about themselves? Can you provide any explanation for this?

Portia
Portia's relationship with her father was obviously very important to her. Although she makes it clear that she does not care for the terms of his will, she is prepared to carry out his wishes with only a few complaints.

2 Imagine that, shortly before his death, Portia's father had told her of his plans and showed her the three caskets, together with their contents. Portia is not happy with the idea of a lottery for her hand in marriage. In the argument that follows, both of them put forward their own point of view – Portia's father defending his scheme and Portia trying to talk him out of it.

Working in pairs, write a script for the argument. Once you have finished, present your scene to a small group and ask for their *constructive* comments on what you have done.

Remember, you should concentrate on the persuasive powers that these two people possess. They both have good reasons for either liking or disliking the idea of the lottery, and it is your task to convey these reasons clearly.

▣ Write a detailed character study of Portia showing how she obeys the restrictions placed upon her by society, but yet still manages to preserve her own individuality and independence.

Shylock

▣ At one point in the play we meet Shylock's friend, Tubal. Although Tubal remains very much in the background of the action, we know that Shylock trusts him and is prepared to borrow money from him in order to secure his bargain with Antonio. We can assume therefore that Tubal has known Shylock for some time. He too is a Jew and so, perhaps, can sympathise with Shylock's grudge against the Christians.

Imagine that Tubal writes three letters to a friend living elsewhere in Europe. The friend has never met Shylock.

- The first letter should be written soon after the beginning of the play. In it Tubal describes the nature of Shylock's bargain with Antonio and, for his friend's benefit, describes the clever money lender who has dared to set a trap for the Christian. The description should be both of Shylock's physical appearance and his general character.

- The second letter should be written after Jessica's elopement. Tubal describes how Shylock is coping in the face of this disaster. (If you want to check the facts for this letter reread Act 3, scene 1.) He should also mention Shylock's growing obsession with Antonio's bond.

- The third and final letter is written after the trial, and in it Tubal describes the effects of the ordeal on his friend. He might also offer his own opinion of the verdict!

▣ Write a detailed character study of Shylock describing and discussing his attitude towards his religion, his money, his family and Antonio. Finish your assignment by writing about your own reactions to Shylock. Do you like or dislike him? If you feel that you cannot totally condemn him for his actions try to explain why you feel this way.

6️⃣ Imagine that Jessica goes to see her father after the trial. Write an account of this meeting. Will there be a reconciliation or will Shylock blame his daughter for what has happened to him?

7️⃣ Write a series of diary entries that Shylock might have made during the course of the play. You will need to show his hatred for Antonio, his despair and rage when Jessica leaves and his anticipation of the trial. What will his final entries reveal?

Antonio

In many ways Antonio is the key figure of the play. He is, after all, *the* merchant of Venice, and without his agreement with Shylock there would be no main plot. Despite this, he remains something of a puzzle. Why is he sad at the beginning of the play? Just why is he so willing to risk his life for his friend? We never really discover the answers to these questions, and at the end of the play, Antonio is still alone; an isolated figure standing amongst the happy couples who people the stage.

The mystery of Antonio's motivation is one that many people have tried to solve. Various explanations for his behaviour have been put forward, including the suggestion that perhaps he himself is in love with Bassanio. In the end, however, we have to accept that Shakespeare has not given us any clear answers to the questions that surround this man. Your ideas, *as long as they are based on evidence that can be found in the text*, are as valid as anyone else's. With that in mind try the following tasks.

8️⃣ It is the night before the trial. Antonio does not know that Bassanio will be there, and he is resigned to his fate. The jailer has provided him with a pen and paper, and so he sets out to write one last letter to his friend.

Reread the letter that Bassanio receives in Act 3, scene 3, to give you some ideas, and then write this last letter. You are going to have to be very careful to make sure that you get the tone right (too much sentiment could easily appear ridiculous), but this is an ideal opportunity for Antonio to explain some of his actions.

9️⃣ 'At no point in the play does Antonio engage our sympathy. Even the drama of the trial scene revolves around the clash between Portia and Shylock; the ultimate fate of Antonio almost becoming a side issue.' Write an essay saying to what extent you agree with this statement.

Antonio and Shylock

10 It is very easy to forget that Shylock has a genuine grudge against his enemy. In Act 1, scene 3, Shylock describes his treatment by the Christians, and in doing so manages to paint an unpleasant picture of Antonio.

Working from Shylock's speech, write a scene showing this meeting. Once you are happy with your script, try acting out this confrontation in small groups. Modern productions have had the moneylender literally dripping with spit!

When you have finished the drama say whether this exercise has altered your opinion of Antonio in any way. If so, how?

Bassanio

11 Working in small groups, compile a list of the characteristics every hero should possess. You may draw on modern films and books for ideas as well as classical tales such as the story of Jason and the Argonauts.

When you have finished your list compare it to those drawn up by other groups and add any ideas that may have escaped you.

Now write a character study of Bassanio, showing exactly how he meets the requirements of a hero. What characteristics does he lack? Does he possess any faults and, if so, are they unheroic? (There are some faults, like a bad temper, that are often displayed by traditional heroes.)

12 Imagine that Bassanio has agreed to give an interview to a popular magazine. The interviewer is anxious to discover as much as s/he can about the man who is to marry Belmont's most famous heiress:

- How did Bassanio first meet Antonio?
- Why does he turn to his friend for money?

- Where are the rest of his family?
- Does he really love Portia or does he just want her for her money?

Try working as a real journalist would, and record your interview straight onto tape. (You will need to work in pairs for this.) Once you have your interview on tape, write it up as a magazine article, complete with title, space for pictures and an introduction.

Nerissa

13 Imagine that Nerissa has kept a diary recording events in Portia's household. Write the entries that she might have made during the course of the play. Remember that she gets engaged halfway through the action. Bassanio is quite rude about Gratiano in the first act. How does Nerissa see him?

14 Although Nerissa acts as Portia's confidante in the play, thus enabling us to find out what Portia is thinking and feeling, she very quickly takes on a life of her own. Write an essay showing how Nerissa's character is firmly established in the few scenes in which she appears and try to assess her importance in the play as a whole.

15 Imagine that Nerissa is talking to one of her grandchildren in years to come. The child has asked how Nerissa and Gratiano first met and she tells the story, continuing it beyond the end of the play.

Write her account of events. You will need to decide whether she remains in Portia's service and which couple wins the bet they make in Act 3, scene 2.

Jessica

16 What was life like for Jessica growing up with Shylock? When did her mother die? How does she feel about her father? When did she first see Lorenzo, and when did she fall in love?

Imagine that Lorenzo and Jessica are talking (another night in the garden perhaps) and that Jessica tells him about her childhood. Write the story of her account.

Launcelot

⚄ The glare of publicity surrounding the trial touches everyone who has been connected with the main characters in whatever capacity. Launcelot becomes a minor celebrity (and a source of great amusement) to the Venetian public. Imagine he appears as a guest on an early evening chat show, answering gossipy questions, nothing too intellectual. He is asked about his part in events and what his opinions are.

Write the script of the interview, trying to keep some of the humour of Launcelot's character. Remember also that he is not the brightest of individuals!

When you have finished you could try staging the best script. Perhaps you could even video it, with the majority of the class playing the audience.

Themes

On page 256 you were asked to look out for the themes of *The Merchant of Venice*. In groups share your findings so far. You may want to add other people's ideas to your own but do not do this unless you can really see how such ideas form part of the themes of the play.

Money

In many ways the play traces a change in the main characters' attitude towards money. If you compare Act 1, scene 1 with Act 5, you will see that by the end of the play money is definitely no longer as important as it was when Bassanio said: 'In Belmont is a lady richly left.'

This change of heart, however, escapes one person. Throughout the play Shylock's attitude towards money remains constant – it is the only thing that he truly loves. If you think that this is a harsh judgement then look again at the speech where he says 'I would my daughter were dead at my foot, and the jewels in her ear' (Act 3, scene 1). Even when he has a premonition that something is about to go wrong, it is his moneybags that he dreams of.

⚀ Try to place yourself in Shylock's mind and then attempt one of the following tasks:

- Describe the nightmare about the moneybags.
- Write a poem that captures his feelings towards his money.
- Shylock is sitting late at night counting his money. Write a monologue setting out his thoughts and feelings.

Justice

With the main scene of the play taking place in court, justice is clearly a central issue in *The Merchant of Venice*.

▨ As a group, re-enact the trial scene in modern English. You should attempt to improvise rather than rely on dialogue that you have written out beforehand. Once you are satisfied with your drama take one of your major speeches and write it down – revising it where necessary.

▨ Design the front page for a Venetian newspaper giving details of the last dramatic day of the trial. Make sure that you choose the facts that you report and the language that you use carefully, so that your readers know exactly whose side you are on. It is unlikely that you will be on Shylock's side unless you are writing for a Jewish newspaper.

▨ Find examples of other courtroom dramas, either in books you have read or in films. (*The Winslow Boy* by Terence Rattigan, where the trial is reported rather than seen, and *To Kill a Mockingbird* by Harper Lee, which shows a trial through a child's eyes, could both be used for this.) Take one of these examples and compare it with *The Merchant of Venice*, discussing the strengths and weaknesses of each scene. Which courtroom drama provides the most powerful images for you and why?

Prejudice

▨ There are several examples of intolerance and prejudice in the play. Using these as a starting point, write a discursive essay setting out your views on this subject. You may wish to confine yourself to commenting on religious intolerance, or you may wish to widen the scope of your essay by considering other forms of prejudice that exist in the world today. Make sure that you explain as clearly as you can why you feel the way you do about this subject.

6 In Act 1, scene 3, Shylock says: 'sufferance is the badge of all our tribe.' With this in mind, research a particular period of the Jewish people's history, and show whether or not this statement can be applied to what you have learnt. It would be most useful to find out exactly how Jews in England were treated in Shakespeare's time.

7 How do you think the Jewish community in Venice will react to the outcome of the trial? Imagine that a meeting has been held to discuss the terms imposed on Shylock. Following this meeting a document summarising the discussion and setting out any action that is to be taken is circulated to the community. Write this document.

8 Over a period of weeks collect examples of incidents showing prejudice from a variety of newspapers. Your examples could include sexism, ageism and racism, as well as religious intolerance. Use your collection as the basis for a class debate on the nature of prejudice.

Mount the articles into a display.

Love

There are at least three types of love that can be seen in *The Merchant of Venice*:

- romantic love
- the love of friends
- the love of family.

9 Design a chart showing which types of love link the various characters. You may include Portia's father in the chart, although he never appears in the play.

10 Write an essay explaining how love appears as a major theme of *The Merchant of Venice*, and show which particular type of love is, in your opinion, the most important.

11 Literature is full of examples of people who make great sacrifices for love. As an open study or wider reading project find two other books or plays where love is the main theme of the work. Compare the treatment of this theme in all three works, saying which you prefer and why. Suitable books for this assignment include *Jane Eyre* by Charlotte Brontë, *Wuthering Heights* by Emily Brontë, *Tess of the d'Urbervilles* by Thomas Hardy, *The Great Gatsby* by Scott Fitzgerald, *Silas Marner* by George Eliot, *The Cone Gatherers* by Robin Jenkins and *The Fifth Child* by Doris Lessing.

12 Write your own story based on the idea of having to give something up for love. Your story can be tragic, serious or comic. You may even want to recount a personal experience.

13 Imagine that Bassanio, Gratiano and Lorenzo each give their wives the gift of an anthology of love poetry. Each anthology has an emphasis that is characteristic of the giver's own view of love. Bassanio's collection will probably stress the importance of fidelity in love, Gratiano's will have a distinctly sensual emphasis, whilst Lorenzo's will be unashamedly romantic.

Compile one of these anthologies, using poems by as many different poets as you can find. A good place to start looking for suitable contributions is amongst Shakespeare's own sonnets, but do not stop there! Remember that these anthologies are intended as gifts so you should take great care with their presentation.

Appearance and reality

14 The riddle of the caskets shows us that it is foolish to accept things at face value. There are several points in the play where people's actions or their appearance are also misleading.

Construct a chart that lists some of these examples. One half of your chart should contain a description of the 'apparent' truth, whilst the opposite side of the chart should describe the 'real' truth. Disguises are obvious examples to start your chart with, but do not forget to pay close attention to Act 5, and what is said there about certain characters' behaviour.

15 Write your own story based on the idea that 'all that glisters is not gold'.

The language of the play

▓ Take Portia's famous speech about the nature of mercy (Act 4). First learn it by heart, then recite it. Now imagine that you have the job of passing on her ideas to a modern audience. Write out your own version of what she says. Bear in mind that you are not being asked to translate the speech word for word, but to provide an up-to-date version of what she says.

When you have finished, get together in groups and compare your different speeches. Decide which you think are best and why, and then go back and look at the original. How do you feel about your speeches compared to Shakespeare's? What have you learnt from this exercise about 'translating' Shakespeare?

▓ Read the following sonnet carefully:

Let me not to the marriage of true minds
Admit impediments. Love is not love
Which alters when it alteration finds,
Or bends with the remover to remove:
O, no! it is an ever-fixèd mark
That looks on tempests and is never shaken;
It is the star to every wand'ring bark,
Whose worth's unknown, although his height be taken.
Love's not Time's fool, though rosy lips and cheeks
Within his bending sickle's compass come;
Love alters not with his brief hours and weeks,
But bears it out even to the edge of doom.
If this be error and upon me proved,
I never writ, nor no man ever loved.

(Sonnet 116)

Discuss how many of the ideas contained in this poem can also be found in *The Merchant of Venice*.

▓ Many of Shakespeare's works display a typically Elizabethan love of puns, *double entendre* and other word games. Using examples from the text show how such word games are used in *The Merchant of Venice*. How would you respond to a critic who argued that these lines should be cut from the play as they can no longer be appreciated by a modern audience?

The play in performance

1 Explain how you would stage a production of the play so that the *differences* in the two settings of Venice and Belmont were apparent to an audience. Think carefully about costumes, the use of music and lighting and exactly how you would design the set. When you have decided how you would go about staging a production, compile a folder with both written instructions and illustrations to show your ideas.

2 In groups, choose one short scene, or part of a long scene, that you feel capable of performing for the other members of your class.

Investigate different ways of presenting this scene. You will need to experiment with grouping and movement within your acting area, the pitch and delivery of the speeches, and ways of conveying the subtlety of the verse to your audience.

Once you have rehearsed sufficiently stage a 'mini-drama festival' and decide which group has given the best presentation.

3 Take a very small extract from the play (three or four pages is quite enough) and consider how it could be filmed. Remember that you should be trying to add to the meaning of the text, not detracting from it by making your camera angles and cuts very noticeable. When you can 'see' your extract in your imagination devise a storyboard as a permanent record of your ideas.

4 Design either a new book cover or a video cover for *The Merchant of Venice*. You will have to provide a short piece of writing for the back of the cover that will tell people something about the play and convince them that they really do want to read or watch it.

You should take great care with your presentation for this assignment. Remember that it is the small details that are convincing. Do not forget to provide a publisher's logo, price and bar code for your book, or a certificate and estimated running time for your video.

5 Design and produce a programme for a new production of *The Merchant of Venice*. As well as a cast list, your programme could contain a summary of the play, a discussion of its relevance to a modern audience, a brief guide to its historical background and a resumé of Shakespeare's career. You will also have to think carefully about a design for the front cover.

Study questions

Many of the activities you have already completed (pages 253–278: before, during and after reading the play) will help you to answer the following questions. Before you begin to write, consider these points about essay writing:

- Spend some time deciding exactly what the essay question is asking. It may be useful to break the sentence down into phrases or words and decide what each part means.

- Focusing on the areas you have decided are relevant, note down as many quotations or references to the play as you can think of which are relevant to the answer.

- Decide on a shape which you think will be appropriate for the essay. It may be useful to think of a literal shape which will suit the argument.

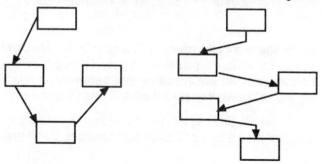

- Organise your ideas and quotations into sections to fit your shape; you could do this by placing notes into different piles.

- Write a first draft of your essay.

- Redraft as many times as you need to, taking care to consider the following:
  Does this answer the question?
  Is this essay easy to read, with clear organisation in which one point flows on to another?
  Do the opening and concluding paragraphs seem clear and linked to the question set?
  Are there any spelling or grammatical errors? Use a dictionary and thesaurus.

1 To what extent does Shylock deserve what happens to him in *The Merchant of Venice?*

2 Choose two minor characters and, with careful reference to the text, show how they are important in the play.

3 'Money is the root of all evil.' To what extent do you agree that this saying is relevant to *The Merchant of Venice?*

4 'In *The Merchant of Venice* Shakespeare shows us that he shares the universal hatred of the Jews that existed in his time. Shylock has no redeeming features.' How true is this?

5 'The true "hero" of the play is Portia. Compared to her the men are ineffectual characters.' Describe Portia's role in the play, showing whether or not you agree with this statement.

6 'The story of Lorenzo and Jessica is superfluous to *The Merchant of Venice*, and the play would be a more powerful piece of drama were it to be removed.' Discuss.

7 Using specific examples from the text examine Shakespeare's use of verse and prose in *The Merchant of Venice*. You will need to show where different kinds of writing can be found and exactly what effect is achieved by changing from one to the other.

8 Explain how changes in our attitude towards 'moneylending', and the experiences of the Jews in the Second World War might make *The Merchant of Venice* a difficult play to produce. What arguements would you present to someone who claimed that the play is no longer relevant?

9 '*The Merchant of Venice* is a play without a hero.' Discuss this statement with careful reference to the roles played by Antonio and Bassanio.

10 'At first sight the scenes containing Launcelot Gobbo appear to be irrelevant to the main action of the play. Closer study reveals that they do, in fact, contain insights into the motivation of the main characters.' With this statement in mind discuss the comic element of *The Merchant of Venice*.

11 The difference between appearance and reality is fundamental to *The Merchant of Venice*. Explain some of the ways in which this idea is used in the play.

12 It has been argued that *The Merchant of Venice* would be a better play were it to finish at the end of the court scene. What arguments can you present both for and against the inclusion of Act 4, scene 2 and Act 5?

Using part of the text

Below are two suggestions for using just a part of the text of *The Merchant of Venice*. You do not need to have read or seen the whole play in order to complete them.

▓ A Fair Trial?

The trial scene of *The Merchant of Venice* is one of the most famous pieces of Shakespeare. In it, Shylock, a Jewish moneylender, comes to court because he has lent money to Antonio, a merchant, and Antonio has not repaid him. He does not want the money but instead wishes to cut away a pound of flesh from Antonio's body, as was agreed in the legal document they drew up.

- In a group of nine, read through Act 4, scene 1, lines 1–396, with eight people reading the parts and the ninth reading the stage instructions.

- On a large piece of paper work as a group to decide where each person is to stand in the scene and how the court might be laid out. Having done this, position yourselves in order to act out the scene. The ninth person now becomes the director. Act through the scene once.

- On your second run-through you should know, in general terms, what is said so you could ad-lib the scene, or even learn some of the words by heart. The characters or the director could add in some additional actions for characters: in some productions Shylock prowls around the courtroom stabbing his knife in the air, and each of the characters would of course react to this.

- Now return to your planning page and decide what costumes you want your characters to wear. You could get together these costumes and even have a go at making some props or items for the set to match your production.

- In your next run-through act your scene out to an audience and get the director to notice which parts of the scene the audience finds exciting or boring. In a final run-through, parts which did not work can be cut and additional exciting pieces added in.

- Make a suitable programme for your performance to give to the audience.

You could also look at some other scenes from Shakespeare in which characters are 'put on trial' in some way, and carry out the same tasks with them. Here are some to look out for:

Act 2, scene 1 of *A Winter's Tale* where Leontes accuses Hermione of having an affair with another man.

Act 5, scene 2 of *The Taming of the Shrew* where Lucentio, Hortensio and Petruchio test out their wives to see which is the most obedient.

Act 3, scene 3, lines 34–97 of *Othello* in which Othello tries to test Desdemona to see if she is unfaithful to him.

2 A Clever Riddle

Portia's father has ordered that anyone who wishes to marry his daughter must solve a riddle and thus choose between three treasure chests, one gold, one silver and one lead. Several suitors try to guess which chest will win them Portia, but they all fail, until Bassanio arrives to make his choice.

- In a group of five, read through Act 3, scene 2, with four people reading characters and the fifth reading stage instructions.

- As you can see, the riddle holds the clue to which is the correct answer. You could read through Act 2, scene 1, Act 2, scene 7 and Act 2, scene 9 to see how some of the other suitors got it wrong.

- Write your own riddle which appears to have more than one possible answer and explain the correct reasoning behind it as well as the mistakes that people might make.

- Test your riddle out on other people in the class. If it is too easy, redraft it so that it is harder to solve.

Longman Group UK Limited,
Longman House, Burnt Mill, Harlow,
Essex CM20 2JE, England
and Associated Companies throughout the world.

First published 1992
This hardback edition first published 1994

Editorial material set in 10/12 point Helvetica Light Condensed
Produced by Longman Singapore (Pte) Ltd
Printed and bound in Great Britain by
Butler & Tanner Ltd, Frome and London

ISBN 0 582 24593 1

Cover illustration by Reg Cartwright

The publisher's policy is to use paper manufactured from
sustainable forests.

Longman Literature
Series editor: Roy Blatchford

Novels

Jane Austen   *Pride and Prejudice*   0 582 07720 6
Charlotte Brontë   *Jane Eyre*   0 582 07719 2
Emily Brontë   *Wuthering Heights*   0 582 07782 6
Charles Dickens   *Great Expectations*   0 582 07783 4
F Scott Fitzgerald   *The Great Gatsby*   0 582 06023 0
                         Tender is the Night   0 582 09716 9
Nadine Gordimer   *July's People*   0 582 06011 7
Graham Greene   *The Captain and the Enemy*   0 582 06024 9
Thomas Hardy   *Far from the Madding Crowd*   0 582 07788 5
                   Tess of the D'Urbervilles   0 582 09715 0
Aldous Huxley   *Brave New World*   0 582 06016 8
Robin Jenkins   *The Cone-Gatherers*   0 582 06017 6
Doris Lessing   *The Fifth Child*   0 582 06021 4
Joan Lindsay   *Picnic at Hanging Rock*   0 582 08174 2
Bernard Mac Laverty   *Lamb*   0 582 06557 7
Brian Moore   *Lies of Silence*   0 582 08170 X
George Orwell   *Animal Farm*   0 582 06010 9
                   Nineteen Eighty-Four   0 582 06018 4
Alan Paton   *Cry, the Beloved Country*   0 582 07787 7
Paul Scott   *Staying On*   0 582 07718 4
Virginia Woolf   *To the Lighthouse*   0 582 09714 2

Short Stories

Jeffrey Archer   *A Twist in the Tale*   0 582 06022 2
Susan Hill   *A Bit of Singing and Dancing*   0 582 09711 8
Bernard Mac Laverty   *The Bernard Mac Laverty Collection*   0 582 08172 6

Poetry

Five Modern Poets   edited by Barbara Bleiman   0 582 09713 4